Living the Mentored Life

Other Titles
By Connie Ragen Green

Rethinking the Work Ethic: Embrace the Struggle and Exceed Your Own Potential

Doing What It Takes: The Online Entrepreneur's Playbook

Book. Blog. Broadcast. – The Trifecta of Entrepreneurial Success

Write Publish Prosper: How to Write Prolifically, Publish Globally, and Prosper Eternally

The Transformational Entrepreneur: Creating a Life of Dedication and Service

Living the Internet Lifestyle: Quit Your Job, Become an Entrepreneur, and Live Your Ideal Life

The Inner Game of Internet Marketing

The Weekend Marketer: Say Goodbye to the "9 to 5", Build an Online Business, and Live the Life You Love

What is Your Why?

Time Management Strategies for Entrepreneurs: How to Manage Your Time to Increase Your Bottom Line

Huge Profits with Affiliate Marketing: How to Build an Online Empire by Recommending What You Love

Membership Sites Made Simple

Article Marketing: How to Attract New Prospects, Create Products, and Increase Your Income

Targeted Traffic Techniques

Huge Profits With a Tiny List: 50 Ways to Use Relationship Marketing to Increase Your Bottom Line

Living the Mentored Life

By
Connie Ragen Green

ISBN Paperback: 978-1-937988-35-7
ISBN Kindle: 978-1-937988-36-4

Hunter's Moon Publishing
http://HuntersMoonPublishing.com

Interior Design by Shawn Hansen
Cover Design by Shawn Hansen

Dedication

For Raymond Aaron, for helping me to shift my thinking and my actions by introducing me to the concept of living the mentored life.

For Denise Wakeman, for showing me the power of leveraging my ideas into writing that would resonate with readers all around the world.

For Armand Morin, for guiding me to confidence and creativity and mentoring me to great success with my business.

For Dr. Jeanette Cates, for taking me to the next level as an online marketing strategist.

And for Joel, who is just beginning his journey with living the mentored life.

Download a Companion Online Course at:
http://LivingtheMentoredLife.com

Foreword

In 2012 I realized a long time dream to visit Machu Picchu. Deciding to trek to the historic Inka site vs. taking the popular tourist train, I knew I would need help. I did not strike out on my own hiking in the Andes. Yes, I probably could have figured out where the trail started from my base in Cusco, Peru. And yes, I could have done a lot of research about what to bring and how to navigate the ancient Inka trail.

And, it would have taken a lot more time, been more difficult and I'm not sure if I could have reached my destination in the time I had.

Instead, I hired a guide. A Peruvian man who had grown up in a small village in the Andes. A man who had been hiking in the Andes his entire life, and leading trekkers for 10 years. He knew the trails. He knew the obstacles, he knew the flora and fauna. Over seven exhilarating days, I hiked through gorgeous landscapes, learned a lot about myself and what I was capable of, and experienced the spectacular Machu Picchu.

I could not have done this without my guide.

What does hiking in Peru have to do with living the mentored life? Over the past 20 years during interviews on teleseminars, webinars, and podcasts, inevitably the host will ask some form of this question: what advice would you give to someone just starting their online business today?

My answer is always the same.

The fastest path to success is to find a mentor to work with. It will be the best investment you can make in yourself and in your business.

A mentor is a trusted counselor or guide.

If you read *The Odyssey* when you were in high school or college, you met Mentor, a friend of Odysseus entrusted with the education of Odysseus' son Telemachus.

Mentor was the original trusted counselor and guide.

When Connie asked me to write the foreword for *Living the Mentored Life*, I immediately took a trip down memory lane, remembering when I met Connie in 2006. She had joined a business blogging program I was teaching. She was an online newbie who needed a mentor and guide to lead her in the right direction in the new and ever-changing world of online marketing.

Over the years, Connie has diligently followed the path, applied what she learned and turned around to mentor the community that rose up around her. Fast forward to 2018 and Connie has mentored hundreds of new online entrepreneurs, paying it forward.

Connie truly exemplifies what it means to live the mentored life. Both as a mentee and a mentor, she embodies two equally important sides to living the mentored life.

First, is identifying and knowing when the time is right for you to engage with a mentor. Whether it's for your business, a hobby, a trek, your education, or for a cause you care about, mentoring accelerates your growth.

I worked with my first business mentor in 2005. He was not a coach. I say that emphatically. I hired him precisely because my business was not growing the way I wanted it to and he had *already paved the way to where I wanted to go*.

And, this is important. When you realize it's time to work with a mentor, it's critical to find someone who's already "been there and done that." Remember, a mentor is a guide and like any guide you hire, they know the path very well and are there to help you over and around the obstacles you may encounter on the way to your destination.

Working with my business mentor from 2005 to 2007, my business grew. I had a trusted advisor to answer my questions, show me new ways to think about and implement new ideas for my business. There's no doubt, my business accelerated faster than if I had been fumbling around on my own for those two years.

I've worked with three amazing business mentors over the last 13 years and each has helped me find and stay on the right path for the subsequent evolutions of my business.

The flip side of being the mentee is assuming the mantle of mentor. You have a gift to share and taking on the role of mentor for someone who wants to learn from you is an honor.

Again, remember the definition of mentor - a trusted counselor or guide. Please don't confuse mentoring with teaching and coaching. Each are important and useful in their place and are often used in combination depending on the circumstances.

If someone approaches you and wants to learn a new skill set, then most likely you'll be acting in the role of teacher, an expert who can impart the specific information required to learn that skill.

A coach is often considered a "facilitator," someone who can help unlock potential to help one on the path of self-discovery.

When someone requests your guidance in the role of a mentor, you have the privilege of helping your mentee achieve their goals with your wise counsel and experience. You're showing them the way.

Living the mentored life is a joyous way to live. At its core, it's about embracing a growth mindset, a way of being where you are simultaneously actively learning and evolving yourself, as you encourage and guide others to do the same while on their unique path.

I learned a lot from Silver, my Peruvian guide. Not only about Peru, but also about how to guide others, gently and patiently showing the way and allowing personal and professional growth to emerge.

In this book, you have a mentor in Connie for how to live the mentored life. Let her guide you on this exciting and rewarding journey. Embrace your growth and then share the gift with others.

Denise Wakeman
DeniseWakeman.com

Preface

I don't know what your destiny will be, but one thing I do know: the only ones among you who will be really happy are those who have sought and found how to serve.
~ Albert Schweitzer

Thinking back, this is the book I could have written first, before writing any of the others where I went into more detail about my experiences with business and entrepreneurship and the various models that make it work. Perhaps this one *should* have been the first, because without this foundation and these precepts entrepreneurship can be a difficult journey. I was reminded of this recently by one of my own mentors and knew on that day I would want to share this information with you, and that's when I began writing this book.

We recently had a speaker at my Rotary Club in Santa Barbara that set the wheels in motion for this book to come about and unfold in a way that would resonate with and make sense to those who seek a different life from that of the average person. That speaker was Tracy Macuga, the Santa Barbara Public Defender.

The presentation right before had been from our Vocational Avenue of Service Chair, and he was sharing information about a program in Santa Barbara called "Partners in Education". This group was formed in 1977 by leaders in the business and education communities. It grew and evolved into a nonprofit 501(c)3 organization in 2000 and is now administered by the Santa Barbara County Education Office.

Their mission is to connect businesses and individuals with schools and youth-serving nonprofit organizations that serve them, in order to improve public education in ways that support a more vibrant economy, the health of our community and the well-being of local children and their families. The premise is that it only takes one volunteer to encourage, to inspire and to reveal something new, opening the door of possibility for the young person in front of them. This program was to be a service opportunity for Rotarians right in our backyard.

When Ms. Macuga was introduced following the "Partners in Education" presentation, she began by telling us that she would not be standing in front of our group that day had it now been for people like us - community leaders, business owners, and involved citizens who had mentored her and her siblings while growing up. She explained that she was one of five children, and that she had lived in a two bedroom apartment in Chicago's infamous "South Side", an area known for its higher than average crime rate.

Macuga went on to share that even though she and her siblings grew up in less than desirable surroundings, she decided to become an attorney, her brother a surgeon, and that all five of them continue to give back to their respective communities as a way to pay it forward. She said,

"It continues to be the privilege of my life to represent individuals with very few resources facing criminal prosecution and to stand shoulder to shoulder with the tireless advocates who serve and protect our clients by vigorous and excellent representation."

A huge part of paying it forward involves mentoring, and in Tracy Macuga's case that was in perfect alignment to the Mission Statement set forth by the Public Defender's office, which is:

Our Mission is to zealously protect the rights, liberties and dignity of all persons in Santa Barbara County and maintain the integrity and fairness of the American Justice System by providing the finest legal representation in the cases entrusted to us through compassionate and innovative advocacy with care and respect for our clients.

She and her team are hands-on in the community to work closely with the people who are most at risk. That was when it hit me that I came from a similar background and would not have reached various levels of success over the years had it not been for the people who had reached out to mentor me in a variety of ways since I was a young child.

My life's journey began as I grew up in poverty, the only child of a single mother trying to do her best so we could survive. We were homeless twice while I was still in grade school, and by age ten I was looking for ways to make some money to alleviate our situation. Just when things were taking a turn for the worst, it seemed like there was always someone who stepped in to help. This came about in different forms, such as a neighbor offering something that we just happened to need at that moment, or someone from the community reaching out to lend a hand. These people were angels in my eyes and I began to take them for granted.

At age fourteen I entered the work force, first as a hostess at a local restaurant and then as a full-fledged waitress. Two years before that I had begun babysitting for neighbors, helping a friend mow lawns, and even scraping barnacles off boats as a way to make money and help out. Somehow I took on this struggle of earning money in jobs that held no future for me as a personal burden and gave up the notion of asking for and receiving the help my mother and I so desperately needed. Later on I share an experience I had with our family dentist mentoring me in dental hygiene, but other than that I made the choice, whether conscious or unconscious to walk the path of life all alone.

It is my hope that you will read these pages with an open mind and a renewed faith in the power and outcomes that are possible by living the mentored life.

Contents

Introduction

You are braver than you believe,
stronger than you seem, and
smarter than you think.
~ A.A. Milne

This book is intended to make you ponder, to then take inspired action upon what you have gleaned, then to ponder some more, and finally to move forward into territory you may not ever have explored, or thought you might have an interest in for your life and your business. Our focus will be on mentors and how living the mentored life can be a joyous and productive one.

As I was working as a classroom teacher during a twenty year period in my life while I was in my thirties and forties, and simultaneously running my real estate business as a broker and residential appraiser, I most often felt like I was going through my life all on my own. Having the freedom and ability to make all of my decisions without input or restrictions from anyone else was empowering, but many times I felt defeated when I was unable to navigate the waters of my everyday life. But this became my normal way of doing things and I persevered.

Never once did I imagine that my life did not have to be so difficult and that there were others who were willing and capable of helping me to achieve my goals. At various times along the way I had glimpses of this different life through people I came in contact with, and these encounters would become the first steps in my pursuit of living the mentored life.

Fast forward to 2005, and I was at the Real Estate Expo in downtown Los Angeles. A friend and I had decided to spend all day Saturday visiting the booths, listening to the speakers, and picking up as many ideas as we could to help us grow our respective businesses. We split up that morning and agreed to meet for lunch and compare our thoughts and notes.

Three hours later we sat down over ham and cheese sandwiches and soda pop and I don't believe my friend got in one word while I shared what I had discovered that morning.

Venturing in and out of the break out rooms that had been set up on topics ranging from multi-unit properties investing to buying real estate in probate, I caught a few words that did not seem to fit this venue. The man was discussing something about mentoring and the importance of mentors and I was intrigued enough to go in and sit down.

This man was Raymond Aaron and I continue to consider him to be my longest and most influential mentor in terms of helping me to shift my thinking and change my life completely. Little did I know on that spring day over a decade ago that I could have the life I now enjoy.

In this writing I will share what occurred in my life leading up to my meeting with Raymond, and what transpired immediately afterwards to encourage me to stay on the mentored path. It continues to be a joyous one, and one that has forced me out of my comfort zone as I stretch and grow in new directions.

In addition, and most importantly for you as the reader, I will explain how you can benefit from my experiences in a way that will change your life forever if you are willing to seek out and work with mentors who know more than you do and are willing to shape and guide your life experiences in a meaningful way.

Are you ready to take the plunge?

What Is the "Mentored" Life?

A mentor empowers a person to see a possible future,
and believe it can be obtained.
~ Shawn Hitchcock

The idea of "living the mentored life" refers to having a variety of people, knowledgeable in specific areas, help you to achieve your goals. Just as you wouldn't ask your accountant how to adjust the timing chain on your car or your manicurist to help you improve your tennis game, you need to surround yourself with a variety of people who are experts in their specific fields. And even more importantly, you are looking for people who are excited at the possibilities attached to helping you and working with you over a long stretch of time. And lest you believe these people are not in your circle of influence, I'll show you exactly how to find them.

Living the mentored life has brought me closer to people who exhibit and live by a strong work ethic, have experience in very specific areas of life and business that are of interest to me, and demonstrate pure joy at hearing of even my smallest successes. This way of living has opened my mind to exploring unchartered waters and turning over leaves I had previous left untouched, stretching me far out of my comfort zone in the process.

You can begin to live this life as well, simply by seeking out mentors in the areas that you are looking to make improvements and change in for your life. Keep an open mind, be willing to humble yourself to someone who wants to help you, and then do the work to achieve your goals and dreams and change your life completely. I speak from my personal experience when I tell you that this journey to living the mentored life is well worth it.

Whether you are new to the idea of living the mentored life or have already benefitted from your experiences, **I highly recommend that you keep a journal or notebook during the reading of this book to record your thoughts and ideas and to chart your progress**. Please join me in finding out more...

Life On Your Own

Walk on, walk on, with hope in your heart
And you'll never walk alone.
~ Oscar Hammerstein II

Life can be a very lonely proposition, at least if you set it up in this way. If you choose to go through your daily life on your own, without the help and guidance of someone more experienced than yourself and without a strong faith and belief in a higher power, you may regularly find yourself all alone on a planet of more than seven billion inhabitants.

I know what this is like and speak from experience when I say that I went through a period during my late twenties and into my early thirties when I could not surround myself with enough people to shake my feeling of loneliness.

At some point I realized that I was going to have to do things very differently and on a daily basis if I were to enjoy success at any level. But I was not sure exactly what to do. Being willing to do the work and knowing what to work on are two very different things.

This is how it began for me. I was out of college, having graduated from UCLA in 1977 with honors and wondering where to go next. I had wanted to become a veterinarian since I was about twelve years old, but working for two vets during my college years and also volunteering at the zoo made me realize that I could not take the physical pain and suffering I would encounter as a part of this career. So I took a year off after graduating from college and before going on to graduate school to find myself and my place in the world.

During this year, these days referred to as a "gap" year and accepted in the mainstream I worked as a bank teller for a large commercial bank that is no longer in existence. It was called Security Pacific Bank and in 1992 it merged with Bank of America in what was at that time the largest bank merger in history. But I digress.

Working at the bank made it necessary for me to focus on my work instead of on myself. This is an important point I'm making here, because giving service of any kind to others, whether it is at a job or in your business, for someone you know who needs help, or with volunteering to assist individual people or in a group project is the secret to clarity and focus. Ponder on this belief and make some notes that will help you to get the most out of this book.

Surrounded with so much cash and inundated with financial documents, it was impossible for my mind to wander during my work day. During the first month the branch manager acknowledged that I was working hard and promoted me to a position of more responsibility as a merchant teller. This meant that I worked with another merchant teller in the "cage", an area separated from the other tellers and only unlocked to bank personnel and recognized merchants from our branch.

I enjoyed the challenge of this position and did my best to complete every task in a professional way. Even though I was only paid about ten dollars a week more in this position than I had been paid as a regular teller, it suited me at that time and gave me a purpose for this time in my life.

One day three masked men came into the bank and forced their way into the "cage", a locked area meant for local merchants to be served with their daily banking needs. They caught me by surprise as I was counting money at the time, but when one of the men grabbed me and held his gun to my head I just froze. The steel barrel of the gun was cold and hard on my face and neck and he twisted my arm in a way that made me cringe and cower away from him.

The entire event took less than ten minutes and ended when I was able to unlock a box in the vault that held more than a hundred thousand dollars. It was a surreal experience in that time seemed to stand still and all of our movements were in slow motion. I have since read that this is typical of such a traumatic and frightening event in our lives.

Needless to say, I decided to end my banking career soon after. But that day is forever imprinted in my mind. And it was on that day that I felt more alone than ever before.

Over the next seven or eight years I tried to find purpose by losing myself within my day to day life; spending time with people I met, traveling, figuring out what I was now interested in doing with my life in terms of a career, going on to law school, taking another job, entering an MBA program, and finally a master's program in instructional technology (I did not finish any of these three graduate programs) and also working at a string of uninteresting, dead end jobs where I was left at the end of each day feeling more empty than the day before.

By age thirty I was no more focused than I had been a decade before, and certainly was not aware of having a life purpose. That all changed on the morning of January the twenty-eighth, 1986 at eight-thirty in the morning on the West coast where I live. It was a Tuesday, and I remember this because I was then working in a small real estate office. Our weekly meeting was at nine each week and I am always running a little bit early.

As I entered the office from the parking lot behind the building I was aware of first the silence, and then of a small group of people gathered around a television set. Immediately I remembered that this was the day the Challenger Space Shuttle was being launched. This was the twenty-fifth shuttle mission and this time the crew included Christa McAuliffe, the high school teacher and first American civilian selected to go into space as part of NASA's Teacher in Space Project. I had always wanted to be a teacher, but my life had taken other directions.

I joined my fellow real estate agents in front of the small television set and within about ten minutes there was liftoff. It was exhilarating to see the space capsule make its way into the sky. All eyes and cameras were on the Challenger and I imagined that I was one of several millions of people around the world watching it live on that morning.

But less than two minutes into the flight that morning, seventy-three seconds to be exact, we all watched in horror as the space shuttle broke apart and disintegrated in front of our eyes. At some point they switched back to Christa's mother and father, watching from Cape Canaveral in the crowd. I won't ever forget the looks on their faces. The media had the good sense not to show her nine year old son and six year old daughter, children who did not grasp what had happened immediately, thank God.

Then they switched to the auditorium at the high school in Concord, New Hampshire where Christa McAuliffe taught social studies, American history, law, and economics. They panned around the room and I looked into the faces of the young people who had known her as Mrs. McAuliffe. In that moment I was enveloped with joy and love, and a feeling of commitment and purpose, and my life changed, in that I made a silent vow to return to school to earn a teaching credential so that I could have an impact on the young people in my community. Following through on that promise and commitment I made that morning, I enrolled in a teacher credentialing program at a university not far from where I lived and in less than one year I was teaching school on an Emergency Credential while completing my coursework to be fully credentialed.

Little did I know that in that moment and with that decision I would begin a journey that would lead me to the mentored life, one in which all things are possible and where you are never alone.

Preparing for Mentorship

Every great achiever is inspired by a great mentor.
~ Lailah Gifty Akita

They have a saying in the southern part of the United States that I truly love. It's "fixin' to get ready" and means that you aren't quite ready to do a thing and need more time. When I researched the origins of this popular phrase I learned that it comes from the need to prepare extensively and make sure everything is perfectly in place before undertaking a new project or goal.

To this I say you must make the commitment and get on with it and preparing to be mentored is no different from any other goal you wish to achieve.

I was a perfectionist for most of my life. Of course, I did not realize this and it was only when I became a foster parent that a social worker pointed it out to me. We were doing the final walk through to make sure my house was ready to receive a child who needed a home while their family was doing what they needed to do in order to bring their child back home in the future.

At one point in this process the social worker turned to me and said, "You are a perfectionist. You must understand that these children are coming from extremely chaotic and dysfunctional living situations and they will not be able to live up to your standards and expectations."

Immediately I became defensive and told her that I was not a perfectionist, and that should be obvious because nothing in my home or in my life was perfect. I waved my arms toward a messy bookshelf and desk with folders stacked up and papers askew.

But after a minute I thanked her for her comment and told her I would give what she had said lots of thought and consideration. My theory was that if someone I respected made a comment of that nature to me, the least I could do was to investigate further. Upon closer inspection I realized she was correct in her observation and that I needed to do some personal work to discover what would come next for me.

This conversation occurred during 1993 and it would take me until 2005 to embrace the concept of living my life in search of excellence, instead of almost always seeking the elusive perfection I craved. I came upon a quote by Vince Lombardi, a member of the Football Hall of Fame and among the top three most winning American football coaches in the NFL that I have taken to heart. It is:

"We will chase perfection, and we will chase it relentlessly, knowing all the while we can never attain it. But along the way, we shall catch excellence."

Once I was willing and adamant about discarding my habit of perfectionism a whole world of opportunity opened up for me. Finally, I was free of the chains that had bound me for almost half a century. Completing projects and moving forward became a way of life. Others accepted me, flaws and all, and I was overjoyed. Replacing the goal of chasing perfection with that of pursuing excellence changed me forever.

It was only then that my first mentor appeared. Or, I should say that it was then that I recognized someone in my life as being the person who could guide, advise, and mentor me. But this was just day one of my journey, a path filled by unexpected twists and turns that I would travel forever once it all came together.

The little voice in my head slowly began to disappear. You know the one I'm talking about here; it's the little voice that tells you that you are too young or too old, not smart enough, not attractive enough, not deserving, and not enough of a person to achieve your goals. Thank that little voice for sharing and then move forward confidently in order to live your best life. You do deserve it, and only you can stop yourself by giving in to any limitations you have set for yourself over your lifetime.

Once you give up the resistance, the rubber band snaps and you are finally free to accept the gifts of the universe. This will be nothing short of miraculous and may rock you back on your heels while you regain your balance. Then the real work begins.

You must roll up your sleeves and dig in, knowing that the course you choose to follow will need correction on a regular basis, the work will be messy, and much of the time you must rely solely on faith to take you to the next steps.

Seek Out Enlightened Individuals

Somehow I knew that I needed to maintain faith, even though the path to mentorship would be wrought with twists and turns. First of all, even though I was ready for my first mentor, I did not have this thought or even the concept in my mind quite yet. What I needed was a spiritual bridge to get me from where I was in 2005 to closer to where I wanted and needed to be. That bridge would consist of individuals who were already in my life, at least peripherally.

But where to find such individuals, that was the question. Being an introvert, I did not have a large circle of friends and acquaintances to call upon for help in this matter. But I did have a small circle of friends and trusted associates that I turned to during that time, in the spring of 2005.

One was a woman named Alicia who ran an exclusive private school at her home not far from where I was living at that time. A year before I had seen a flyer at the local public library looking for a science and technology teacher a couple of days a week. On an impulse I had called the number and connected with Alicia and her school. She turned out to be a kindred spirit, someone who had taught in the public schools and had become disillusioned with the way in which many children and their families fell through the cracks. She returned to school and earned a degree in Educational Therapy and then opened her own school from her home the following year, with the help and encouragement of her husband and two adult sons.

I'll share more of the story of this chance meeting and the impact it had on my own life, as well as the lives of more than a dozen teenagers that year later on in this book, but for now I will simply say that our friendship was key to my transformation during this period of my life.

On this particular day I called Alicia and asked her if she knew of anyone she could introduce me to who had changed their life dramatically and significantly away from the world of teaching and education. Unlike me, Alicia was a social butterfly and enjoyed interacting with many people on a regular basis. I just knew she would have a name for me.

In fact, she had two names. She briefly described a couple she had known for years who had reinvented their lives during the previous year. I was anxious to meet them and she arranged a meeting the following week.

My Eyes Are Opened And I Am Fully Awake

Yolanda and Vincent were very different from any people I had met during my lifetime. She had worked in corporate America for the previous twenty years, while he had worked in commercial real estate during that same time period.

We agreed to meet at their home, not far from where I was living at that time. When I arrived at seven in the morning as they had requested, their day was already in full swing. Yolanda greeted me at the door with a warm smile and genuine hug, as did Vincent a moment later.

They welcomed me into their home and did not ask me many questions, choosing instead to share their lifestyle with me as a way to elicit questions and responses. Vincent dashed into the kitchen, tugging at my sleeve to follow him and threw open the refrigerator, outstretching his arms as if to present the contents and smiling broadly.

"We have only natural and organic food, and it spoils rather quickly," he exclaimed.

Yolanda was right behind him, opening each of the cabinets and the drawers in order to expose the contents of each of them.

"Everything you see here represents the way we have changed our lifestyle over the past two years. We care about the environment, sustainability, and keeping our bodies and home clean and pure. It is part of who we have become since we left the work force."

I wasn't sure what to say, except that I admired them for taking a stand on something they felt so strongly about and sticking with it for so long. Then I mumbled something about how this might be simpler without kids at home and when you have enough money to make these kinds of choices. This was my limiting belief showing up and attempting to convince me that other people could achieve goals that I could not.

They glanced quickly at one another before gently guiding me to sit me down at their dining room table. Yolanda and Vincent proceeded to school me about the possibilities of life. At some point their two teenage children appeared and joined in the discussion. I was amazed at their enthusiasm and willingness to make such drastic life changes at the suggestions of their parents.

All of the assumptions I had made about Vincent and Yolanda were just that, and they showed me what it meant to make decisions that were so closely aligned with beliefs and to follow through with them, no matter what the consequences or the cost. I knew I had made friends for a lifetime and I hoped to be able to share something helpful with them in return in the future. Little did I know that this wish and belief would not be necessary or required.

The Catalyst

I would have to say that spending time with this couple was the catalyst for change in my life. They renewed my faith in mankind and restored my childlike enthusiasm and anticipation of great things to occur in my life on a regular basis. Over the following months I learned so much from this couple and their children, it was as though I had enrolled in a doctorate program on life essentials.

Pursue Mental Toughness

It was from my friend, mentor, and colleague Joe Vitale that I first became aware of something referred to as mental toughness. In 2005 Joe had interviewed a man who had started something he called the Mental Toughness Institute. I no longer remember the man's name and his group is not around these days, but the concepts and strategies shared during that interview have remained in my consciousness to this day.

We have all heard about people who overcame great obstacles in their lives and emerged victorious. The ones that come to mind are people who were POWs (prisoners of war) in wars and conflicts, those kidnapped and held captive for years, and people who found themselves at odds with the government, the medical community, or with the law who believed so much in their cause and its outcome they were willing to devote much of their lives to not only making it through their situation but also devoting the remainder of their lives to making sure others did not have to go through a similar situation. These people exhibit the traits, qualities, and characteristics that define mental toughness.

One family I knew personally was that of Adam Walsh, a boy who was abducted from a department store near where I was living in south Florida during the early 1970s. His father, John Walsh, became an advocate for victims of violent crimes and was the host of the television show *America's Most Wanted*, a weekly program devoted to finding missing children that ran for twenty-five seasons. I spent time with this family over many years and wondered if I would have the courage to do what they were doing to help others in similar situations after their precious six-year-old son's life was taken in such a violent manner. They looked inward to determine what they were made of and then developed the mental toughness habit to persevere and move forward with their lives.

The Walsh family organized a political campaign to help missing and exploited children. Despite bureaucratic and legislative problems, John's efforts eventually led to the creation of the Missing Children Act of 1982 and the Missing Children's Assistance Act of 1984.

Today, Walsh continues to testify before Congress and state legislatures on crime, missing children and victims' rights issues. His latest efforts include lobbying for a Constitutional amendment for victims' rights.

So, where do we begin with this? Mental toughness is defined as being a measure of individual resilience and confidence that may predict success in sports, education and the workplace. As a broad concept, it emerged in the context of sports training, in the context of a set of attributes that allow a person to become a better athlete and able to cope difficult training and difficult competitive situations and emerge without losing confidence. In recent decades, the term has been commonly used by coaches, sport psychologists, sports commentators, and business leaders.

It turns out that the level of your mental toughness is directly related to your daily habits both intuitive and acquired over time. Few people are aware of this. Instead, they think that being mentally tough is something you were born with. Because it is not an inherited trait, you can easily develop and improve your mental toughness over time.

I have formed habits that serve me well, such as writing each day and connecting with influencers regularly. Let's define a habit as being a routine that you follow each day, almost without thinking about it consciously. No one has to tell you to brush your teeth each morning and evening, because this activity has become a habit.

What about mental toughness; how high would you say your level of mental toughness is right now? Answer the following questions and add this to the journal or notebook you are keeping as you read this book:

Do you give up on a new task when it gets tough?

Do you find reasons and excuses for everything?

Are you are stuck in accomplishing a specific goal, regardless of what you do?

If you answered yes to any of these then your mental toughness needs working on. When you allow excuses to stop you, you are only hurting yourself. It is not really your lack of motivation or willpower it is your lack of mental toughness. The good news is that you can change this, and rather quickly I will add.

What are the benefits and how will this help you as you prepare to be mentored through life? When you have mental toughness you do not allow obstacles or excuses to block your way. Instead you battle through regardless of any situation or circumstance, despite how intense it may be at the time.

Now if mental toughness is directly related to your daily habits, then the easiest way to improve your mental toughness is by developing and improving your habits. Choose one thing that you want to become a habit and work on it. It only takes about twenty-one days for a habit to become engrained in your mind. That really isn't that long now if you think about it, is it?

If you want to drop a few kilos (the European way to say lose a few pounds) but haven't given up added sugar yet, this could be the place to begin. Get tough mentally and stop doing this so that you can more easily achieve your goal.

Another example is wanting to run in a 5 or 10K race but you haven't yet. Identify and determine what it is that is stopping you and think about how badly you want it. If you honestly want to achieve this with all of your heart and soul then you will achieve it. You will find time to fit in your training runs and this will fill you with a sense of great accomplishment.

What all of this comes down to is how determined you are to excel in your daily life. To reach the level of success you desire you simply need the perseverance to keep on going. This means scheduling and planning out your runs and putting tools into place so that you succeed.

To become a mentally tough person you need to be willing to stay true to yourself. This entails not going off track and being willing to find a way to get things done. If you do get diverted from your path for any reason, take the time necessary to course correct and get back on track. And I promise that along with this will come increased confidence and higher self-esteem. Not bad when you consider that this will make a difference in every area of your life.

The Next Logical Step

A dream you dream alone is only a dream.
A dream you dream together is reality.
~ John Lennon

As you begin to embrace the concept of living the mentored life, I want you to ask yourself this question on a regular basis:

What's My Next Logical Step?

When thinking about mentoring and how this process could change your life, you must ask yourself this question and be prepared for the answer. What I mean with this is that reaching your goals is never going to be a one or two step process. Your dreams are much greater than that, and you must have a more detailed plan to carry you through to completion. And be willing to honor and embrace the struggle that comes along with goals of great meaning and value to your life.

Please note here that I said you need a "more detailed plan", not a complex plan. Simple is best and has opened the doors of great success for me over the years.

So what exactly is the next logical step for you, and how do you know if it's the right one for what you wish to achieve? Would the next logical step be the same for someone who wanted to change jobs as for someone who wanted to quit their job and start a business? The answer is yes. Allow me to explain.

When I wanted to leave the school I was teaching at back in the early 1990s and find a new position at a different school, I needed to first make a list of what I liked and didn't like about my current position. Then I thought about exactly what I wanted as a classroom teacher and sought out the best people and resources to assist me.

Years later, when I wanted to leave classroom teaching completely and start my own business, I made a list of what I liked and what I did not like about teaching in the classroom. Then I thought about exactly what type of business I wanted to start and sought out the best people and resources to assist me with this decision.

So you can see that making a list of the pros and cons of your goal comes first, followed by finding the right people and resources to help you make your decision. I believe that many people skip over these two steps, making it next to impossible to chart a course for their journey to achieving their goals and dreams. Step back and make sure you are getting started in a way that will support what you wish to achieve.

The next logical step will depend upon many things, including where you are currently, in relation to your goal and how you envision the final stages of this journey. This is where a mentor can make all the difference with how your life takes shape and you move closer to where you would prefer to be.

In my example of wishing to leave my job as a teacher and start an online business as an entrepreneur, I needed guidance and training around what an online business could look like for me. Instead, I set out on my own and got lost in all that was available at that time. I spent thousands of dollars on products and courses that did not take me any closer to my goal. It was only when I found and hired the right mentor that my business took off and I was able to see my goals and dreams falling into place.

Your mentor will be your advocate, seeing things from their perspective and unfolding your options out to you in a way that will convince you it was your idea and intention all along. Your mentor takes you under their wing and places opportunities in front of you at the proper time. Your mentor pushes you out of the nest, and then opens their arms wide to catch you if you begin to fall. And, most importantly to me, a mentor teaches you to be grateful for and to appreciate what you already have in your life so that you may be open to receiving even more.

Your mentor will guide you to the next logical step in your journey to success, so trust them and see what's possible. But first, allow me to share the questions you may ask yourself in order to discover your passions.

Questions to Ask Yourself to Discover Your Passions

If you're lucky, you have already discovered many of your passions and get to spend much of your time enjoying things that bring you excitement and joy. However, maybe you've not yet connected with activities, skills, and interests that ignite your passion.

It takes time, soul searching, and some life experience to identify your true passions. These prompts are written to tap into your wants, needs, desires, and fantasies. Have fun with them and discover what you can add to your life that will fill it with delight.

What's the one thing I have always wanted to do? Consider what would need to happen in order for you to carry through with this long sought after wish. Make a plan, create your strategy, seek out a mentor, and then get started.

If I could spend today doing whatever I desire, what would it be? Let your mind go. It could be something related to your work, your home, or simply a lark.

Where do I really want to live? What city and what type of residence?
Perhaps you are already fulfilling this passion and you do live in your true first choice locale. If not, ponder the possibilities of moving to a new location you'll love.

Where would I like to visit?
Perhaps you're harboring a secret yearning to visit Washington, D.C. or Yosemite or Westminster Abbey in London. The streets of Sydney, Australia or Hong Kong may be calling your name or even the Grand Canyon or the canals in Venice, Italy.

How can you make it happen in a reasonable period of time?
What do I talk about doing but never do it? In a conversation, you might state something like, "For the last twenty years, I've really wanted to take a cruise to the islands of the Caribbean to explore the lifestyle and to get to know the people."

What are some of the reasons I don't go after my dreams?
Explore within yourself why you haven't pursued the life you want. Can you do something differently beginning today to help bring your dreams to life?

How will I finish the sentence, "More than anything, before I die, I want to _____?"
Say it out loud and fill in the blank. Then, figure out a way to accomplish your wish.

What are the things in my life that I would like to get rid of?
If you're discovering you don't love everything about your life, maybe it's time to do some "housecleaning." Make a list of the ways you would like for your life to change.

Which people in my life inspire me and why?
It's important to know who inspires you so you can spend more time with them. What is it about them that lights you up so much? Decide to take every step to be inspired more often.

If I were to make just one radical change in my life right now to make life better, what would it be?
Your answer to this question will really open up your possibilities. Moving to a bigger city might really spice up your life. Getting more education or starting a business, at least pert-time might be a goal...plus you'll likely make more money.

You'll be happier if you chase your dreams. Make one change.

How do I feel when I put all my effort into accomplishing one of my goals?
Notice these feelings. You will no doubt want to experience them more often and this is possible if you really want it badly enough and are willing to make some changes.

How do I feel whenever I achieve a life goal?
Awesome, probably.

What's missing from my life?
Answering this question requires considerable soul-searching.

Who are my biggest supporters?
It's wise to know the people that will stand behind you and help you pursue your passions, no matter what.

Who gets in the way of me achieving my goals?
In order to find your true passions, you might be required to disengage from those who wish to counteract your efforts.

If you take the time to thoroughly ponder each of these questions, you'll be pleased with what you discover. Your true passions are inside you, just waiting to be let loose to bring you excitement, joy, and fulfillment.

Why is Mentoring Important?

A mentor is someone who allows you
to see the hope inside yourself.
~ Oprah Winfrey

Having someone mentor you is an exercise in letting go of past limitations and negative beliefs. Once a more experienced person takes you by the hand and guides you towards the actions required for you to achieve your goals, you have a clarity, focus, and vision that is unparalleled.

For example, I wanted to write an eBook when I first came online but didn't have the first idea of how to get started. I was overwhelmed with too much information on the topic, extraneous information on related topics, and my own lack of confidence and experience. I didn't know what I didn't know, which is typical when you are just starting out in a new field.

Then I reached out to someone who was an expert in this area of writing, publishing, and marketing eBooks and everything changed. He mentored me for a few months and my writing came together quickly. While I was writing he began sharing by example how I would publish and market my eBook. I continued to work with him on this project and within six or seven weeks my first draft was completed. I was soon able to achieve my goals and even to teach others the process I had gone through to reach the point I was at right then.

I thought back to my years as a classroom teacher and remembered how I would ask my students to help each other with complex, multi-step concepts. Once a student "got it" he or she was in the unique position to teach another student who was on the verge of a breakthrough in understanding the concept themselves.

Mentors and mentorship are integral parts of the success process. In my opinion and based on my personal experience I will tell you that a mentored life is one in which anything is possible. Always wanted to write a book? The right mentor can help you to do this in record time. Need to lose some unwanted weight? Again, a mentor can show you the way. Wish to leave your "9 to 5" job and become an entrepreneur? Living the mentored life gives you steps to take and a path to follow as you begin your journey.

A mentored life is truly a life fulfilled. By interacting and collaborating with people who have both general and specific knowledge in the areas you wish to master you instantly get on the fast track to moving your life forward in the desired direction.

I can remember back in 2005 listening to a recording of a session my first mentor had just finished with a man who had started a successful real estate company with franchises all over North America. I thought my mentor had asked me to listen to this interview because of my background in real estate, but that was not the case. The conversation turned to the topic of volunteering with local non-profit organizations and within a month I had become a part of the Rotary Club, an international service organization that takes on local projects as well as those throughout the world, in my city.

My mentor had the wisdom to know that this was a direction that would change my life in ways that would not be apparent to me for at least a couple of years. This alone is an excellent reason to pursue mentorship in your life. Having someone take you under their wing and lead you to new, life changing experiences is something that most people in the world will never understand. A mentor can help catapult you to a life you currently cannot even imagine. You owe it to yourself to find out more about living the mentored life.

The Places You'll Go

You have brains in your head you have feet in your shoes.
You can steer yourself any direction you choose.
~ Dr. Seuss

This quote from the wonderful and amazing Dr. Seuss sums up just what is possible when you allow yourself to live the mentored life. Go ahead, read the quote again, this time out loud, and allow your voice to take on a sing-song tone and your body to move with the rhythm of the phrases. The possibilities are endless and the journey a joyous one.

Why isn't this kind of life possible when you're walking the path on your own? Because two or more heads are always better than one and the little voice in your head can sometimes sabotage your greatest goals and grandest dreams. Mentors change all of that, sticking with you to make sure you don't get derailed by anyone or anything.

Time Proven Concept
What I am sharing here is not new or unique to entrepreneur. In fact, it's one of the oldest concepts in the universe and can be traced back to Biblical times. Most often mentorship was described in terms of Kings and fathers passing down wisdom to trusted allies and sons, but you can be sure that women were also a big part of the mentorship process from early times.

My own mentors describe their early mentors with great love and admiration. One shares a story of how he was almost forty, overweight, and heavily in debt when his wife asked him for a divorce. They had a young daughter and the thought of not living in the same home while she was growing up was almost more than he could bear. He began searching for answers and wasn't sure where he should turn.

He soon met a man who would become his first mentor, even though he was not familiar with that term or the process at that time. Over the next two years he came to an understanding with his now ex-wife that allowed him to see his daughter whenever he wanted to, he got out of debt completely and increased his child support and alimony payments to his family, lost forty pounds in a healthy way, and became happier than he had been in many years.

When he shares this story, people always want to know exactly what it was that his mentor did for him. They are seeking a formula or a step by step blueprint that would include the secrets to success. Of course, it wasn't that simple for him or for any of us.

Another of my mentors shares a story of suffering a debilitating injury that left him in a wheelchair and unable to bend his legs for a four month period. As he went through numerous surgeries and his muscles atrophied beyond his control he knew that he had to depend on the guidance of his mentor to come out victorious on the other side. It was humbling to have other people care for his basic needs and to have to rely on his faith, inner strength, and mental toughness to make a full recovery. He did so and is now a thought leader in the area of fitness and nutrition who works with professional sports teams and testifies before Congress to share his wisdom and experience.

Think of the process of mentorship as an ongoing and evolving journey that requires ongoing introspection and massive action. It all begins with the first step, which is to acknowledge that life is a team sport that requires interaction with people on various levels and in a multitude of disciplines. You will start with a single mentor who will assist you in an area of great interest and concern to you at this time on your life, and then expand to include additional mentors for the areas you also want to learn more about and include in your journey. Once you relax into this new way of thinking, believing, and living your life will begin to pivot in a direction that might amaze you.

Great Mentors

Oprah Winfrey often spoke of Maya Angelou as being one of her greatest mentors. She said, "She was there for me always, guiding me through some of the most important years of my life."

These stories go on and on, and I will share some of the ones I have deemed to be most relevant with you throughout this book. But for now, let's focus on the possibilities for your life experience if you choose to live the mentored life.

Your Mentored Life

Years ago I had neighbors whose daughter was about three years old when I first moved into the neighborhood. This little girl was quite charming, wearing long blond curls and an impish grin you could spot from half a block away. But she was wild, screaming at the top of her lungs when she didn't want to do something or things didn't go her way.

She also had a mischievous streak, which exhibited itself at the most inopportune times. Once, when she was about five she decided to feed my dogs. She showed up at my front door with a plate of hot dogs and sauerkraut and when I opened the door the chaos began. My dogs, a basset hound named Abigail and a dachshund named Jack quickly rushed forward, knocking the girl and the plate of food to the ground. It was a mess, with all of us covered in food and I ended up walking her back across the street and delivering her to her parents. Did I mention that I was entertaining two couples at my house when this occurred?

Over the years I observed how this child's mother and father mentored her, along with a carefully chosen handful of other mentors. She had a music lesson once a week, joined a soccer team at the local park, and had a reading tutor when she needed that specialized help in her studies.

Over time the wildness was curtailed, all the while allowing her to express herself freely. She joined a children's theatre group one summer, and I attended their final performance. The long blond curls were piled atop her head, and the familiar impish grin morphed into a beautiful smile.

She was accepted into a magnet school, and the mentoring continued. During her high school years I watched as she became an asset to her school's orchestra when she took up the violin, and received first place honors for an essay she composed.

A difficult child became an accomplished young lady, with the help of caring mentors who guided her in directions that made sense and were a good fit for her gifts, talents, abilities, and interests.

And you may be wondering what part I played in all of this. The truth is that I was a very different person all those years ago, so my role was as the kind neighbor who was willing to offer a ride when needed and was invited to participate in birthday parties and attend recitals and other school programs.

I have no regrets, as we are all exactly where we need to be at any given time. It's all a part of our life's journey, and up to us to explore the possibilities of taking it further.

What about your possibilities? There is no limit to what you can achieve when you are mentored. Olympic and professional athletes typically employ mentors to give them an edge and an advantage over others, as do Fortune 500 CEOs, actors and others in the arts, and even people like you and I. Make a list of your wildest dreams and ask yourself what you would love to accomplish if you had an insider's perspective and guidance. What could you achieve if you knew you could not fail? **Imagine the possibilities and write them down in your journal or notebook.**

Serving Others

The best way to find yourself is to lose yourself
in the service of others.
~ Mahatma Gandhi

Living a life of service is a joyous existence. And once you begin your life's journey of living the mentored life, you'll be prepared and willing to give this service by mentoring every person you come in contact with each day. This is tantamount to waving a magic wand of blessings over almost everyone you encounter. This happened to me recently when I was speaking at a conference and was able to gift my course on how to write a book to several people I was able to work with in a group on one of the days we were together.

American author H. Jackson Brown reminds us to "earn your success based on service to others, not at the expense of others."

Whether it's by showing someone which buttons to select when they are new to using ATM machines outside of the local bank, or spending time with someone to help them choose the next career they will pursue, a life of service can be the most satisfying and rewarding one you can live.

A century ago in Europe and Scandinavia a life in service, primarily working for wealthy families was considered to be as important as teaching or nursing. Both young men and young women aspired to this calling that took them away from their families for most of each year. Of course, this wasn't the perfect career and lifestyle by any stretch of the imagination, but the concept was a worthy one.

The mentored life teaches you to provide such service as you are called to do and have a heart for so that many others' lives are touched in a most personal way.

And just as stated by Mahatma Gandhi in the opening quote for this chapter, service to others is the path to moving further away from your own troubles as you help others with their situations and circumstances.

As a younger person I did not understand this concept and I was not around anyone who could show me the way. I can remember conversations I had with my fellow teachers when they questioned why I spent my recess period refereeing my fifth and sixth graders' basketball games.

My response to them was, "I dare you to think about your troubles, or anything else for that matter while you are running up and down the basketball court while the ball is in play."

What I would come to realize later on was that by being of service to the kids I was fully involved in what they cared about and my thoughts of problems, some of which would never actually occur were lost and finally dissipated.

What About Luck?

Often I feel as though I am the luckiest person on planet Earth, but is it really luck? In my business world, I am surrounded by awe inspiring people who continue to help me grow as an entrepreneur. I have colleagues, clients, students, and joint venture partners I am so honored to know, mentors who guide me to what is best for my personal goals, and people in my community who hit reply just to tell me how much what I do online means to them.

What I'm describing here isn't luck. Instead, it's the common, modern definition of luck...where preparation meets opportunity. I continue to prepare myself each day for the opportunities that will avail themselves to me. It is simply a matter of living full out and of keeping my eyes and ears open to opportunities and possibilities.

The smartest thing I did when I began in 2006 was to start blogging. But before I went very far in this direction I found a mentor to assist me in this area. Her name was Denise Wakeman and I am proud to say that I still know her and continue to learn from her to this day. She was kind enough to accept my invitation to write the foreword for this book after I told her she was the only person I thought of whose message would resonate so deeply with my readers on this topic of living the mentored life.

Denise and a partner had started on online training course and forum where I was able to explore the concepts they were teaching on the topics of blogging and visibility, as well as connect with the others who were in various stages of creating a business around the written word and with a blogging platform. I flourished in this virtual setting and found my voice.

Before I began working with Denise in this course my writing left much to be desired, I wasn't sure what I could write about, and I lacked clarity with my goals. If I didn't know where I wanted to go as an online entrepreneur, how could I write for others?

With the help of Denise, a caring and knowledgeable mentor, I moved past the doubt, the fear, the feelings of inadequacy, and just started writing. And as soon I found my voice, clarified my message, and began enrolling my tribe, I was the author and publisher of a simple little blog that people read and resonated with and that I write for to this day.

Now I maintain two blogs and have grown them into what we refer to as "authority sites" that are read across the planet by those who want and need information, resources, guidance, and more on the topics around entrepreneurship and personal development. And I have grown right along with my readers.

My blogging led to my first published book in 2010, *Huge Profits with a Tiny List: 50 Ways to Use Relationship Marketing to Increase Your Bottom Line*. This book was a compilation of fifty blog posts from my "Huge Profits, Tiny List" blog. It quickly became a bestseller and catapulted me to a level of success as an entrepreneur that had previously eluded me. This was an excellent example of my preparation meeting an opportunity and having it all perceived by many as good luck on my part. I knew better, and have continued to be lucky in my life as well as in my business as I work smart, rather than hard each day.

My writing, in all forms and formats becomes a way to better serve those who resonate with my message of entrepreneurship by choice for a life you love and deserve. Each time I begin a new post, report, white paper, video, podcast, audio recording, or book I first think about who I am writing to and how what I share will serve them at the moment we connect. And I never forget that without a mentor to help me, I would not have been able to achieve this level of success and deeper insight.

Inspiring Others

Inspiration is one of those concepts that eludes us until we feel and experience it on a personal level. I was in college at UCLA when I was first aware of being inspired by another human being, to the point that I could feel it in my mind, my body, and to my very core.

The year was 1977 and the speaker was both an activist and an economist. His name escapes me now, but his message moved through me in a way I had not previously experienced in my young life. His talk was on the topic of investment in companies that conducted business in South Africa, in protest of the apartheid system. I was so naive on this topic that I had to listen closely just to get up to speed on the controversy. It wasn't as though I could Google it from my smart phone right then, as we are able to do today.

An hour later this speaker had completely won me over to his side, the side that I could not imagine anyone else on the planet not committing to wholeheartedly. When someone reaches into the depths of your soul, enlightening you and rearranging your beliefs and values to match your core beliefs, it stays with you for a lifetime.

Since that time I have been inspired by many people around a whole host of issues, and at some point people began to tell me that I was inspiring them. I was taken aback at first, and then dissected it to realize just what they were referring to here.

It was my story that had moved and resonated within them, and that's when I understood the power of storytelling in our lives. My business has experienced great success in part due to these stories. Some are about me and others are about the people and situations that touch my heart.

Most recently, I was inspired by the people involved in two, unrelated events. The first was the now infamous "debris flow" in the Montecito area of Santa Barbara.

I wasn't in Santa Barbara on January ninth, 2018, but I was supposed to be there early that morning. Because I live in two California cities, Santa Barbara by the ocean and Santa Clarita in the desert, as well as travel extensively for both business and pleasure, my time is divided and always subject to change. I had a dental appointment on that morning, but something prompted me to cancel it just days before. I've given much thought to why this happened and feel that God was warning me to stay away at that time.

The rainfall was expected and anticipated, as southern California has been in extreme drought for more than five years now. What was not expected was the record amount of rain that fell, and the subsequent "debris flow" (this is the politically correct term for a mudslide) that followed.

As the massive boulders worked their way into the community of Montecito and towards the ocean in the early morning hours, the streets became impassable and the freeway disappeared under the deluge of water. It was only hours later that day it was discovered that many people had been swept away during the height of the storm. Twenty-four people lost their lives on that day, and hundreds more became heroes. Over the next couple of weeks the stories unfolded and we learned of heroic acts that not only saved lives but defined the people who were a part of them. One person pulled a baby from under the mud after hearing a faint cry. Another carried an elderly woman on his back to higher ground.

These stories inspired me to be a better person, someone who is always on the alert to help another in need. It seems as though it takes a catastrophe to teach us that we are all in this life together, doing our best, rising above the odds, and working together to do and create the improbable as often as possible.

The other, unrelated event was an off-site lunch meeting set up by our Rotary Club president on Valentine's Day, where we met at a local company that hires developmentally disabled adults to perform work for small businesses in the community. We were introduced in their large meeting room, and I think all of us were a little nervous in the beginning.

Then we went outside and had a bar-b-que lunch of pork sandwiches and all of the fixings. While we sat down to eat the Club president handed out Valentine cards to everyone, each with a name on it. The idea was for the Rotarians to each be paired with one of the people working at the company in order to foster friendship, fellowship, and more.

My card had the name "Mario" on it, and as I carried my plate to the trash can I asked some of the people working there which one he was. They pointed towards a man sitting all alone, wearing a plaid flannel shirt and smiling. I came up and introduced myself and sat down beside him.

For the next half hour Mario and I became friends. We shared a little about ourselves and it turned out Mario was also watching the Winter Olympics from Pyeongchang, South Korea that week. He is a part of the Special Olympics in Santa Clarita and plays soccer and runs track as his events.

Mario so inspired me that day. His family disappeared before he was an adult, so he has made the best of it by adopting the people around him as his family. He lives with other adults in a group home and looks forward to coming to work each day to see his friends and co-workers, and to earn some money. I'd like to tell you that all of the Rotarians took the time and initiative to get to know their special person that day, but many people have a fear of the unknown and snuck out early. I would not have missed this experience for the world.

When someone in my life tells me that I have inspired them, I am quick to say thank you and acknowledge them for being there for me. I am grateful and thankful each day that someone somewhere in the world is motivated to take action, to execute what they have learned, and to further change their life as a result.

Who inspires you and whom have you inspired?
It turns out this is an important part of our life's journey and something mentors will make a part of the work you are doing on yourself and in your business.

Think of the stories you could share to allow those around you to better understand issues and topics you care about. **Answer these questions and add them to your journal or notebook.**

What If You're Mentored?

*Self-esteem is a huge piece of my work.
You have to believe it's possible and believe in yourself.
Then you need to seek out role models and mentors.*
~ Jack Canfield*

What if you choose to live the mentored life; will it be a significantly different experience than going through your life on your own? The short answer is yes, it will be quite different.

When you choose to live the mentored life, doors will open and possibilities you did not even know existed will show themselves in the light of day. Your self-esteem and confidence will increase, to the point that you will believe you can have, do, and be anything. Why? Because it's true. If I achieve nothing else with the writing of this book, it will be to convince you wholeheartedly that you are capable of creating and living the life you desire and that only you can hold yourself back from achieving your dreams and goals.

In this section I'll share just what is possible in your life experience and journey, and how you can enjoy even greater benefits and results by following some simple, yet highly effective strategies in a focused and organized manner.

And please understand that once you have a taste of the mentored life you are not likely to go back to what you did before. Maintaining the status quo is not anyone's goal, when you get right down to it with them in a serious discussion.

Then I'll share the concept of "lifestyle design" and how you can achieve your goals and dreams simply by starting with a solid vision of what it is that you do want from yourself during this lifetime.

Asking the question "What if?" on a daily basis will expand your mind and allow you to daydream in a way most of us haven't done since we were young children. It's that childlike wonder upon which innovation soars, creativity runs wild, and miracles occur. Being a part of this style of thinking, acting, and believing is a wild ride and a never ending journey to unlimited, uninhibited, and unbridled potential. Buckle up now and let's take off, together!

Just What Is Possible?

Everything you can imagine is real.
~ Pablo Picasso

Even though I have no regrets whatsoever as to what has occurred and transpired throughout my life experience, it taught me that it's the contrast between what you want and what you do not want in your life that moves your forward. I did choose to learn many things the hard way. This started at a young age, while I was being raised by a single mother who herself had experienced challenges and obstacles throughout her life.

My very first experience with asking someone other than my mother, another adult in my family, or a teacher or someone else in a position of authority about something I needed help with was a dentist my mother took me to when I was about ten years old.

We were very poor and twice annual dental checkups were not a part of my childhood experience. When one of my teeth was causing me pain we made an appointment. Typically it was a new cavity, and by age ten I had eight or so fillings in my mouth. So on that particular day I was at the dentist because of a toothache and I asked the dentist if I had done something wrong that caused this to occur.

I can remember the scene vividly, my mother sitting in a chair next to me in the dental chair, and the dentist standing above me and looking down into my mouth. With my question lingering in the air, he took a step back and waited before answering.

He proceeded to tell me what to do each day to prevent tooth decay, and even though I had been brushing twice a day as far back as I could remember the other instructions and information was foreign to me. At that moment I accepted him as my dental hygiene mentor, though it would be almost forty years into the future before I would understand it in that way.

The results were nothing short of phenomenal. I went for a cleaning twice a year after that, had x-rays once a year at first and then once every two years, and I ceased to have cavities on any regular basis. I did everything he said to do, including brushing in a different way with a different type of tooth brush, flossing after every meal, gargling with a special rinse, and being more careful and aware of my teeth. This meant no more opening up bottles of soda with my teeth or chewing ice, two comfortable but quite dangerous childhood habits I had picked up and fallen into along the way.

The point I am attempting to make here is to show you that you can achieve anything you want in your life, whether it is eliminating tooth decay or starting a new business.

Super You

Mentors have given me super powers over the years, and the wherewithal to attempt challenges and goals I would not have done otherwise. They made the mistakes first so that I could avoid them.

For more than a decade I have been mentoring others in the areas of entrepreneurship and authorship, and this is where I am able to bestow super powers on them in a similar way to what I continue to experience.

Your goal is to listen to and follow the guidance of the mentors you choose to work with in various areas of your life so that the process comes full circle and can be passed on to future generations. Mentorship can be the legacy you carry on and pay forward.

Believing in yourself and going forth each day with an air of confidence gives you a competitive edge in the world. And I know that my telling you to have confidence is not the same as you having that confidence, so please take the time to develop that on your own as I did when I became an entrepreneur.

Confidence means that you believe in yourself and know that you are enough. Tell yourself this every day, and say it out loud regularly to reinforce your new belief system.

Fears that once paralyzed you no longer stand in your way. Go ahead, raise your hand and offer your thoughts and opinions to a group. Face your every fear and do it anyway. What an empowering feeling it is to do something you thought you could never do.

Move forward with your ideas and know that they have validity. Refuse to be stopped by hesitation and insecurity. Second guess yourself no longer. You are strongly tapped into your intuition and common sense and know when to follow a prompting.

Understand and acknowledge that you are a unique individual with special gifts and abilities that will make a difference in the lives of those you encounter.

Time Management Strategies

I believe this is the best time and place within this book to share some time management strategies with you. Most of what is possible in my own life is a result of how I manage my time each day. If you always or almost always feel like your day is getting away from you and that you won't possibly have time for what you wish to accomplish, these strategies will change your life over time.

Get enough sleep each night. It's a known fact that the overwhelming majority of people of all ages do not get enough sleep on a regular basis. The lack of sleep or sleep deprivation accounts for accidents, low performance, illness, and relationship breakdown. If this describes you, take action to change your sleep habits to change your life. Even though I like to watch television shows or Netflix films before going to bed, I limit that to one hour, read for another thirty minutes, and then go to sleep. This allows me to get up early the following morning, refreshed and ready for my day. It would not be possible for me to do as much writing as I do without following this advice almost every single day, with a few rare and planned exceptions.

Create a plan for your life. I use a three year plan and now have my family on board with this strategy as well. You're heard the saying "If you don't know where you're going, you'll end up someplace else." I have found this to be true and experienced the disappointment of a life unfulfilled during my younger days, as I shared with you earlier in this book.

Instead, write down what you wish to achieve and where you would like to be three years from today. Make sure to accelerate the ages of everyone involved, as this makes a difference in almost every area you will explore.

Where will you live, who will you be with, what type of work will you do, who will you serve, and how will you spend your days in three years time? Answering these five questions can change the direction of your life forever. I recommend sitting down once a month for an hour or two to do these exercises, and include your closest family members so they will know what you are thinking.

Chunk it down. Once I knew where I wanted to go in my life and business, I broke it down further into monthly goals. Then I took each month and made weekly goals. I tend to work four or five days each week and know exactly what I seek to accomplish during that time. For example, my goal is to write two original blog posts each week, and I chunk that down into three pieces - outlining my idea for a post, writing the post, and editing and publishing the post. Something will always come up that throws you off track with your scheduled plan, but you will recover nicely if you know that you can make up any lost time and move confidently towards your goals.

Commit to lifelong learning. One of my goals as a classroom teacher in the inner city of Los Angeles was to inspire and motivate my students to continue their educations. Living in poverty in a crime ridden neighborhood lends itself to children growing up much too quickly and leaving the world of education behind. I used myself as an example and told them about the classes I was enrolled in at night while I was teaching them by day. At first they could not believe I did this, but when I told them I didn't *have to*, but instead *wanted to* continue learning they began to understand. One semester I was taking a class in astronomy and shared how difficult the subject matter was for me. My fifth graders came up with interesting ways for me to learn what was being covered, and in the process they learned more about astronomy than our curriculum covered.

Take your office with you. Now this is different than taking your work with you everywhere you go, in that I am referring to always having a few crucial tools in your possession when you are away from home. For me these include my smart phone, a notebook, a pen, a physical book, and a healthy snack. Whether I am stuck in traffic, waiting in line, or waiting for an appointment, I have at my fingertips the tools I need to accomplish some of my goals or at least to flesh out my ideas. Recently I was in a long line at the post office and I read two pages of the book I'm reading currently, answered an email, and went into deep thought about a new product I'm creating with a client. When it was my turn I almost wanted to let the person behind me take my place so that I could continue my productive daydream.

Daydream, meditate, and nap regularly. You must make time for what I refer to as "quiet time" each day. Whereas many people do this first thing each morning, I prefer to do it later on, at around nine or ten in the morning. I find that I can then be more focused on myself and my "inner game" after I have spent a few hours accomplishing some of the tasks, activities, and goals I wrote down for that day. As a classroom teacher I was told to discourage daydreaming in my student's behavior, but I found this activity to be an integral part of the educational process. And I didn't take my first nap until I was almost forty years old and now find them to be enlightening and rejuvenating. Meditation takes some practice, but this ritual allows you to take a mental vacation right at your desk.

Know and believe that anything is possible and achievable in your life. Like the quote from Pablo Picasso I used at the beginning of this chapter, everything you can imagine is real. Sometimes it takes us until later in life to see this concept manifested in a physical sense, so if you can accept it now and feel the power connected to that statement you will be on your way to a life you have previously been unable to imagine. The role of mentors in your life is to gently teach, guide, and encourage you to the greatness that has always been inside you.

This chapter gives you many questions and ideas that you may wish to add to your journal or notebook.

In the next chapter on Lifestyle Design I will give some concrete examples of the areas my mentors have helped me to flesh out into a huge part of who I am today as a human being.

Lifestyle Design

A person's success in life can usually be measured by the number of uncomfortable conversations he or she is willing to have.
~ Tim Ferriss

You are an awesome human being. How do I know this? I know it to be a fact because you are reading this book and have made it almost half of the way through so far. Do you have any idea how many people don't complete the reading of even a single book in one year? The numbers are astounding as well as frightening to someone who makes their living with reading, learning, and writing.

As a former classroom teacher I do not understand how anyone can overlook the great gift of reading and what it can do to further their own goals as well as helping people all around the world to further their own understanding, beliefs, and values. I only taught in the inner city, where the majority of my students were from families who experienced generational illiteracy. They so appreciated the fact that their child was learning to read at an early age, and it encouraged many of them to take adult school classes to learn to read as well.

Until I was forbidden to do so any longer, I used to invite parents to sit in during one of my lessons and to participate in the discussion on the story or topic. When you read, comprehend, and discuss you become more awesome with each story, lesson, and idea that is shared with you by the author. The secret is in the follow up with this learning strategy, which is to write about what you have read, understood, and then discussed.

Now that you have accepted yourself and my belief in you as an awesome human being, know that you have at your fingertips the tools you need to design your life. This is referred to as lifestyle design and has been around since the dawn of time. However, it is only during the past couple of decades or so that so many of us have had the knowledge of how to achieve this in our own lives, thanks in the most part to the work of mentors from all walks of life and from every corner of the earth. Every thought and action we engage in each day is a choice, so my advice here is to choose wisely and to be open to what can transpire.

What Type of Life Do You Choose?

It is a known and accepted fact that we all experience and receive the life we choose. If aspects of any area of your life are not as you wish them to be, you can simply change direction and move closer to your life's goals. I did this when I decided not to complete my final year of law school and instead pursued a career in real estate. I did this once again when I returned to college to earn a teaching credential after being inspired by Christa McAuliffe, the first civilian and teacher in space who perished in the space shuttle Challenger disaster in 1986. And then I made a choice once again when I left my classroom teaching position and my work in real estate to start my online business and become an author, publisher, and entrepreneur. You can do it starting right now. Today you have it within your power to take the first step towards the rest of your life, as cliché as that may sound.

And please do not allow that little voice in your head tell you that other people can have the choice to do this but you cannot because you are...

You fill in the blanks here, because no matter what your current beliefs or feelings of limitation are I will work hard to turn your thinking around. If I can choose a life that is meaningful, rewarding, and satisfying in so many ways, you can do so as well.

Take some time after you finish reading this chapter to write down in your journal or notebook where you are right now in the areas of your life you wish to change, and where you would prefer to be. You may have heard that most people do not get what they want in life because they do not know what they want. When I heard this years ago I got busy deciding what it was I did want as a part of my life experience and what steps and actions I would need to take each day in order for me to achieve my goals.

Imagine your day from start to finish, fleshing out the details in as great a depth as you possibly can. Where in the world are you? What do you see? What can you hear? Who is there with you? What is the weather life? What will you be doing an hour from now and with whom? Think about the smells, tastes, sounds, colors, and anything more you can add to your story to make it as real and as vivid as possible.

I have now practiced this so much and for so long I can hear the ocean waves gently crashing to shore, hear two different species of birds chirping in the distance, smell the toast that is not quite burnt, and feel the warm ray of sun upon my cheek. The colors range from a pale blue to a soft peachy orange and I taste the lemon water I am sipping.

I first did this exercise and achieved great results quite by accident in 2005. After attending an event on success in business, I followed through with one of the activities they encouraged us to do. I am not an artist, yet I was willing to take a piece of blank paper and draw a picture of where I wanted to work. My vision was of working from home in a brightly lit room with a high ceiling. My view was of the mountains and canyons below, and the windows were covered with white plantation shutters. My two little dogs were at my feet, stretched out on their mats and enjoying the ray of sunshine that was coming through the opening between the window and the sliding glass door that led to my balcony with the majestic and scenic view.

Keep in mind that I was still a classroom teacher at this time, as well as working in real estate during all of my waking hours away from the classroom, and that both of these occupations required me to be away from home for at least ten to twelve hours a day, six or seven days a week. During the winter months this meant that I left home in the morning and returned in the evening while it was dark, leaving me deflated as to why I was working so hard to have a home I did not see during the light of day.

Also, I was living in a one story tract home (imagine little boxes that all look very similar to one another) with no view and in an area where there was no open space, save for a few neighborhood parks dotted here and there, meaning that the home I was envisioning could not have been possible in my present reality. Because I was seldom at home during the daylight hours due to the nature of my work, visualizing a better life seemed to elude me. Yet, within one year I had resigned from my teaching job and given away my real estate clients, and my new home office was almost exactly as I had imagined on the day when I had drawn that picture.

And even if I had had the means to build a new home in my former city, there was no open space in which to do so. Somewhere deep in my subconscious mind I was dreaming and imagining and beginning the process of manifestation of something that did not and could not exist where I was living at that time.

It was almost a year after I had moved into my brand new home that I found that original picture. I'm sure my jaw dropped at I sat in my home office and traced over every detail with my right index finger. My dogs were resting at my feet and I could hear birds chirping outside on my balcony. Had I really drawn that picture and manifested this new workspace and home as a part of my life's journey? Yes, I had. I felt powerful yet also very afraid at that moment. Was it really this simple? If so, what else had I created in my life over the years, both positive and negative?

I know for a fact that I could not have come full circle with my ability to use lifestyle design to change and improve my life, as well as the lives of those around me if it had not been for the mentors I connected with. It was in 2006 that I truly understood this phenomenon and made a covenant with God to follow through with this awareness. I further promised that I would become a mentor for others and would seek out the exact people who would help me to achieve the life I want and deserve. Are you willing to do the same?

And as for the quote from Tim Ferriss I shared at the beginning of this chapter, yes, my conversations with the new people I was connecting with became more uncomfortable, more poignant, and more valuable as a way in which to guide me almost seamlessly into the new journey on which I was about to embark.

I am urging you to get uncomfortable as often and in as many ways as you possibly can. You're not looking to pick fights with anyone, but instead seeking out opportunities to interact and experience a different way of creating the life of your choice. The people who know you best will finally say - who is this person and what have they done with the person I used to know. This is a good thing and will lead to much needed change in you and in the people around you.

How Mentors Continue to Guide Me

Mentors enable this process by knowing our strengths and areas that need to be improved and guiding us to success. I've shared that I had always wanted to write, yet did very little writing over the years because I felt inadequate in this area. My mentor explained how I could start with a simple idea, write a few paragraphs about it each day, turn these into blog posts, and then combine them into a book. The result was the first of more than a dozen popular, bestselling books I have written and published since 2010.

I was strong in the "ideas" area but needed to improve in the "writing" area and that has been worth millions of dollars to me during this time. Instead of acknowledging that my writing was mediocre at the time, my mentor gently persuaded me to go down a path that would lead to more time and experience with the writing process, and ultimately a completed book that would change the way I was perceived by the outside world forever. This single action, having me write a couple of hundred words each day based on my ideas, gave me the confidence to move forward in a way I would have said was simply not possible at that time.

Another area I have excelled in with the help of mentors is with thinking bigger and fleshing out ideas that will allow me to continually move to the next level in my business. Even though I understand the concept and the importance of being constantly in upward motion, I know better than to believe I can achieve this growth on my own.

Are you having more thoughts about living the mentored life?

Can you visualize how and why it is so beneficial to share your life experience with another person who can help you to shape your future in a way that will make sense for you? What is the first area of your life you would explore with a mentor? Perhaps it would be your business, but it could also be in the areas of health, relationships, or specific skills such as cooking or selling. I continue to have mentors in all of these areas and continue to grow immensely as a result.

Make more notes in your journal and let's continue to the next section of the book.

How is This Life Possible?

Discipline is the bridge between
goals and accomplishment.
~ Jim Rohn

Up until this point I have shared what mentoring is and how it can be defined, why it is so important to entrepreneurs and others wishing to improve and enrich their life experience to be mentored, and what is possible if you choose to live the mentored life.

Now we will move forward from these precepts and I will share how you can live in this way and change yourself from the inside out. It all begins with communication, an area where most of us continue to struggle throughout our life's journey.

Much of the communication options available to us today was not even thought of when we were children and young adults. And because these are so new, it makes it even more challenging to get our thoughts, ideas, and messages out to others in a way that allows them to understand and respond appropriately. Mentors can and will alleviate some of the pain of miscommunication as you take on this important area of your life.

For example, texting was a means of communication I had not heard of at the turn of the century. In August of 2001 I was visiting my extended family members in Finland and Sweden to attend my stepson's wedding. At some point my stepdaughter's cell phone made a sound I was unfamiliar with and she picked it up and typed something in return to the sender.

This was called SMS (Short Message Service) and allowed her to type up to one hundred sixty characters of text to someone. I wanted to know more and several of my family members spent time explaining it all to me.

When I returned to the States a couple of weeks later I couldn't wait to share this new technology with my friends. No one had heard of it, and the cell phone carriers were not aware of it either. It would take another few years before text messaging would be available and commonplace among the people I knew. But once it was, communication was never quite the same.

After communication comes implementation, where you are willing to risk failure in return for great rewards. Without the action of implementing, communication is just conversation in one format or another that is likely to be lost and discarded very quickly. Implementation makes it part of the permanent record of your life's work and a legacy in the making.

Finally, I'll share how innovation rounds out this trifecta of actions for the mentored life.

The glue holding all of this together is equal parts of discipline and persuasion. After starting my online business in 2006 I became more disciplined with my habits and actions than I ever thought possible. And after much work and implementation I can say with certainty I have mastered the art of persuasion in many areas of my life.

Persuasion is the magic power to enlist others in your ideas, to the point where they are willing to come aboard and explore the possibilities alongside of you.

Think about how your life will be different when you can communicate your ideas openly and get your message across to others, implement what you are saying that is important on your topic, innovate your thoughts and ideas to a higher level, have the discipline to accomplish what you set out to do, and demonstrate the ability to persuade others to join in enthusiastically and be a part of your community. You will be a person to be reckoned with and a thought leader in the making.

For now, write down these words in your journal and a short phrase or sentence to describe what they mean to you:

Communication
Implementation
Innovation

Discipline
Persuasion

These five concepts, taken together in unison and fleshed out into meaningful ideas become the playground and the laboratory of the mind. We'll revisit these at the end of the book for further discussion and investigation.

Finding Your Mentors

Change your thoughts and you change your world.
~ Norman Vincent Peale

The first step in finding a mentor is to take a look at where you are right now in relation to where you would prefer to be. This involves changing your thoughts, something that is easier said than done in the beginning and will become second nature to you over time.

And just like anything else in life, you must make this into a daily habit. Be prepared to backslide once in awhile over the course of your lifetime, but know that once you have mastered this skill you may draw upon it at any time to return to that mental state of being in charge of the thoughts you allow in.

Here is an exercise I do almost every day that will help you to get on the right track here. I call it "The Seventeen Second Rule" but this strategy has been taught by many and shared worldwide under different titles and descriptions.

The Seventeen Second Rule

Our mind is a complex and sophisticated muscle. The more I learn about it the more I want to know. Perhaps this will be a serious field of study for me in the future. For now, I will share with you a concept that was first introduced to me in 2005, while I was attending a series of live events and courses from a group called Peak Potentials that would subsequently assist me in changing my thinking and my life. This group is still active to this day, with the founder's son now at the helm.

The idea here is to hold a pure thought in your mind for seventeen full seconds. This may first appear to you to be an easy request, but even though it may be simple it is far from being easy to achieve when you are getting started along this path. I started out by holding my pure thought (this is a clearly defined thought that is specific to what you wish to achieve) for just a few seconds - seventeen, to be exact, and then moving up from there by doubling it to thirty-four seconds and then to the final goal of sixty-eight second.

This pure thought may be as simple as wanting to do well on an upcoming job interview or as complex as wishing to live in a different city. Nothing you can imagine and wish for is off limits here. By visualizing your goals and then stating your goals out loud, you can rewire your brain to improve mindset, increase happiness and success, and stay focused on your innermost thoughts, dreams, and goals.

Sit quietly in a place where you will not be disturbed. In the beginning I did this in my bedroom or in my home office, and only when no one else was at home. In advance, I had chosen a goal to focus on for that day, and I made sure to keep it simple. I have a clock with a second hand that I used to keep track of the time.

Once those seventeen seconds fly by for you, quickly double your pure thought time to thirty-four seconds and increase the complexity of your goal.

For example, at first my goal was to think about leaving my job and starting an online business from home. Once I could think about only that for seventeen seconds, and without any judgment, plans, or other complicated thoughts, I move on to my thirty-four second version. Here I thought about what my day would be like working from home. Can you see how I shifted my thinking from that of wanting to figure out how I could quit my job and what kind of business I could start to one where I was simply envisioning the ease of getting up when I wanted to and working from my home.

When I moved on to the sixty-eight seconds I would think about the people I would serve as a writer and entrepreneur and the joy that would come to me as a result.

I hope that you are following the progression here, where at first I was more concerned with the details of how to achieve my goals and finally I was enjoying the process of allowing my dreams and goals to unfold in a way that would be joyous and satisfying to me. It was a matter of moving subconsciously from the tactics level on to the strategic stage of designing the life I wanted to live.

And in keeping with the theme of this book, focusing a pure thought on the idea of attracting the right mentor for you is a valuable use of this exercise. I was not even aware that I was searching for a mentor when I first began using the seventeen second rule, but instead I asked God to help me change my life. My prayer was answered when I connected with a mentor.

Who Is The Right Mentor?

You may already have thought about, or even written down in your notebook or journal the question I am most often asked on this topic of living the mentored life. That is...

"How do I find the right mentor for me?"

This is an excellent question, and one that can be answered easily enough once you know what you want in your life. Many times we seek out people to help us, whether they are medical professionals or people who are experts and authorities in specific areas of interest to us, only to discover that we do not know what we want out of life.

Of course, we know the basics about the work we wish to be engaged in, where we want to live, and what we'd like to do in our spare time. Or at least we think we do. The truth is that the career or job you entered while you were in your twenties may have been greatly influenced by the people and circumstances in your life at that time.

Your parents, teachers, friends, and other significant people within your circle of influence most likely steered you to the work you did at that time, even though it may have been subconsciously on their part. We seek to please those we care about, even though this borders on the psychology of why people do what they do, and in so pleasing them we give away more and more of who we are deep inside. And it is so easy to justify our actions for decades to come.

We all know more than one person who took over the family business, remained in the city where they grew up, and married the person their friends and family liked, only to find out much later that this work, locale, or spouse would take them further and further away from the life they would love.

Think back, and be brutally honest with yourself here, to a major life event you experienced that you knew at the time, at least at a subconscious level would not be in your best interest or in alignment with your goals, desires, talents, abilities, and interests. And instead of being angry, bitter, or disappointed with how things turned out, know that it is always within your freedom of choice to turn things around This happened to me when I moved to New York to attend a prestigious law school after graduating from UCLA. It did not ever feel like what I wanted to do, but more like what others expected for me to do with my life at that point in time. Luckily, a turn of events during that first year allowed me to gracefully change the course and direction of my young life before it became almost impossible for me to do so without encountering heartache and expense that would bog me down for years to come.

Now I am not suggesting that you initiate a divorce, sell your home, move to a new location, or quit your job. Instead, I want you to be willing to have the courage and to do the work to enjoy life on your terms with lifestyle design. It's possible, and it's much simpler than you could ever imagine. Your first, or next mentor will help you to get there, and on your terms.

You Already Know This Person

The "right" mentor for you is most likely someone you already know. I find this to be true about ninety percent of the time when working with someone in this area. I will now explain how to proceed in a way that will serve your needs and get you on to the path of living the mentored life.

Think about and make a list of the groups of people who are within your circles of influence. Again , I define a "circle of influence" as consisting of the people you come in contact with on a regular basis who are aligned with similar beliefs and core values as yours. Before starting my online business in 2006 I had a very small circle of influence, and it has grown exponentially over the years. This one piece has accounted for friendships, business, and enlightenment that most likely would not have been possible if I hadn't been willing to connect with others and think of the new relationships in this way. I now have multiple circles of influence, consisting of various and overlapping people in one or both of the communities where I reside most of the time, when I'm not traveling.

When I arrived in Santa Clarita, the desert community in southern California that I moved to in the spring of 2006, very few of the new homes being built were completed. It was also much colder than usual for that time of year so I was staying indoors much more than usual, my head down and working at my computer. I needed an outlet to be with some people once in awhile, so I Googled for what was going on in my new town.

When I typed in "volunteer opportunities in santa clarita" for my Google search, the local Rotary club was in the first few results, along with the Chamber of Commerce and some other groups. I remembered seeing the blue and gold Rotary wheel as I had driven across the United States in years past, but I wasn't sure who they were or what they did. I visit to Rotary.org told me they where an international service organization, begun by four attorneys from Chicago in 1905. They rotated the offices where they met each week, hence the name. Their first service project was to construct a public toilet on the streets of downtown Chicago for shoppers and others in need of these facilities.

It was quite intimidating for me to attend my first Rotary meeting. It was the early summer of 2006 and I was attempting to get my online business off the ground. I had resigned from my teaching position and given most of my long time real estate clients away to those engaged in real estate on a full time basis. So basically I was unemployed. The sound of that didn't hit me until I was walking in to the restaurant where the Rotarians were meeting. What could I say to make it sound more positive, while still being truthful?

Sure enough, the first person I met shook my hand and asked me "What do you do?" Without hesitation I said,

"I am a former classroom teacher and real estate broker, and now I am starting an online business."

It worked! He introduced me to someone else and they got me set up with a choice on entree for lunch. Then I turned around and observed who else had come into the room. The mayor, two people on the City Council, me new veterinarian, my new dentist, and people who looked and seemed very different than myself. It wasn't too late,

I thought. I could leave the way I had come in and forget all about this. But this was what I wanted; to be surrounded by people who thought, acted, and lived differently than I had in my life experience so far. I took a deep breath and stayed.

And in that instant I had done what Norman Vincent Peale suggested in the quote I included at the beginning of this chapter:

"Change your thoughts and you change your world."
By changing my thoughts to positive ones of hope and accomplishments and of dreams realized, I had surrounded myself with sixty people who would become my fellow Rotarians just a few months later. And even though I am now a member of the Santa Barbara Rotary, I continue to spend time with this original group. I even dedicated my first book, *Huge Profits with a Tiny List: 50 Ways to Use Relationship Marketing to Increase Your Bottom Line* to them because of the impact these people had on my life and how they showed me over and over that anything was possible in my life.

Your Morning Routine

Review your goals twice each day in order
to be focused on achieving them.
~ Les Brown

Before we get into the general and specific areas of your life where mentorship will be of great value, I want to address a concept that will make a pronounced difference and allow you to reach new heights in your life. This is your morning routine and how it affects everything you do from the moment you open your eyes in the morning until your head hits the pillow that night.

The precept is that the first hour of your day sets the tone for the following twenty-three, and that we have it within our power to predetermine exactly how this hour will unfold, barring any situations popping up that are out of your control on a given day.

Later on I'll be sharing the effect of negative self-talk in the mornings and beyond, and how this plays a crucial role in your success, but for now let's discuss how to get your day off to an excellent, productive, and positive start.

Possibly the best advice I or anyone else can give you is to tell you that you must plan out your morning routine and then the remainder of your day, the day before. This is the secret; your morning actually starts during the evening before that next day begins. Write this down in your journal before you continue reading.

Leaving your day to chance is not a strategy employed by successful people. I have learned to model the behaviors of people who are living life in a way I want to emulate, and that is exactly what I am sharing with you here.

For most of my life I have lived in a way that was not my idea. What I mean by this statement is that when we are in school and then enter the work force, typically we are living by a schedule not of our choosing or design. Looking back, I could have had more of a say in this matter, but I was too caught up in the day to day challenges and struggles of life. It was only when I began my online business in the spring of 2006, while still working at my classroom teaching job and also as a real estate broker and appraiser that I created a morning routine that would ultimately change my life forever.

Because my time was so limited, as most people's tends to be, I was forced to plan out how I could achieve my goals with the new business while also fulfilling my duties and obligations for work and at home.

My goal was to spend two hours each week learning about something related to my business, and also to write and publish two blog posts each week. On some days it seemed as though I did not have even one extra minute, and when I found some time I was simply two exhausted from my hectic schedule to turn these into productive periods of time.

As soon I gave this dilemma more thought and made it "top of mind" as a priority, the solution presented itself rather quickly. And this led to me finding out something about myself that I had not realized before.

When I began my teaching career people would regularly say to me that it was wonderful I was a morning person. I would always correct them by saying that I was not a morning person, but someone who had chosen a career where it was imperative to be awake and ready to work at a very early hour. But the truth was that I really was a morning person and just had not seen it that way.

During the year that would be my last year of teaching as I launched the online business, I also moved about twenty-five miles north of the city I had lived in for more than a decade. This meant a much longer commute each morning during the final semester. And with traffic as it is in the Los Angeles area, I knew I would have to leave home an hour earlier than I was used to. But the move was a positive one, and I had built this new house and wanted to live in the new community of Santa Clarita.

After experimenting with times to leave in the morning that would ensure my on time arrival at school, I determined that I could leave home at five forty-five and beat most of the traffic, arriving at school by six forty-five, depending upon the traffic flow that day. I would sit in the car in the school's parking lot until about seven, when one or more people had arrived and we could walk in together. Trying to read or write during that time did not work because there was not enough time and once others began arriving I was too distracted to do anything else. The minutes flew by too quickly and I needed to sign in by seven thirty to set up my room and to greet the students arriving by eight each morning.

On the third day of following this schedule and routine, the bright light finally came on; I had about forty-five minutes each day that could be put to much better use than what I was doing currently.

That night I took out my mini legal pad and made some notes. Instead of waiting until I had time to do some work and then deciding what to do and how to make the most of this time, I wrote down my ideas for two blog posts and notes about what I would focus on learning that week right then and there. At that moment I committed to not going to sleep at night until I knew what I would be doing the following morning, both for the classroom and my real estate business. It was amazing how my mindset changed as soon as I did these small things. It was as if I was taking over my life and my destiny for the first time in a long time and this was a wonderful feeling.

The following morning I left at my usual time, five forty-five but on this day I did not park in the school's parking lot. On this day, the first day of my new morning routine I parked instead in the parking lot of the post office a few blocks away from the school. I maintained a rented post office box there to help with transferring my mail to my new city, but had never stayed in my car after picking up my mail in the mornings on my way to work.

As I got into the car a feeling of joy overtook me and I was awash with thoughts and ideas. I took out my notebook and pen and began writing. I had a mobile office! For the next thirty minutes I wrote out one of my two blog posts for that week, ideas for the next two, and even listened to part of an audio recording that was training me how to host my own teleseminars. And because it was relatively quiet in the post office's lot compared to the one at school, I was more focused and productive than ever before.

I recommitted to this idea of not going to sleep until I knew what I would do at school, in real estate, and also for my new online business the next day. This seems so simple, but it was an epiphany for me at that time in my life.

Your Perfect and Effective Morning

I am oversimplifying the concept of a morning routine here, but I want you to understand the power of taking control of your time on this way. The best morning routine for you is the one that works best for your goals, but you may not know where to begin. Here are my thoughts on this.

First, you must define your perfect morning. Where are you, with whom, and what do you have planned for later in the day? Write it down, for if we do not write down what we wish to have, be, do, and achieve during our life then there is little likelihood of it coming to pass.

Once you have defined your goals for your morning, ask yourself how what you are doing now is different than what you have done in the past. Sometimes this is enough to make a significant difference, and other times this is the catalyst to motivate you to change your life radically.

A successful morning routine includes what I call "quiet time" and you may interpret as time for prayer or meditation; focused gratitude for what you already have in your life; reflection of the previous day's events; thoughtful contemplation of today's events; and daydreaming of future events. This five part process can be accomplished within fifteen minutes or so, or drawn out into an hour or even longer. Let's go through each piece of this morning routine so you can decide what fits best into your current life experience.

Your "quiet time" must begin as soon as possible after you are awake. If you are responsible for others in your home and must spend time with them each morning, then setting your alarm to awake earlier may be the only answer. if that is the case, be thankful and do this.

During this quiet time your mind will tend to wander, especially in the beginning. You will be aware of your surroundings and of everything you must do during the day. But get into the habit of pulling yourself inward so that you may enjoy being alive and everything that is possible in your life. Think of positive and happy times, past and present and of how you can be a blessing to those around you. Envision yourself as the powerful human being you are and imagine what you would be capable of if you only had the opportunity to give of yourself freely each waking moment.

Move into the gratitude phase of your morning routine by thinking of everyone and everything you are grateful for, no matter how small. As you run through the list of people, events, and situations, praise yourself for your accomplishments in your life and think about how fortunate you are to be in this position today.

Now think back to what occurred yesterday and reflect on the people who were involved. What did you say and do that was effective and resulted in the outcome you were hoping for and expected? What could you have done differently?

Now think about today, contemplating what you have planned and what you will need in order to make the day a success. Is there something you could do this morning to ensure a better outcome? Role play in your mind the interactions you will have with others. What can you say to someone today that will have a lasting impact on them forever?

Finally, allow yourself to daydream about what could be. This may be the most challenging piece of your morning routine in that most of us stopped daydreaming while we were still children if the adults around us made this out to be something that was wrong or taboo. I will encourage you to find that child within you who believed that all things were possible and that you could be anything you wanted to be in the future. Daydreaming is the most important part of each day in that you are able to suspend reality and simply focus on what you want for yourself and in your life.

Whether you are an entrepreneur, run a small business, have a job or career, or are out of the work force completely, there is a sixth step you will want to take. While you are preparing for your morning routine the night before, write down exactly what you intend to accomplish the next day. Once I did this, my work day went from nine or ten hours, where I was exhausted by three or four in the afternoon, to about four hours each morning and an occasional hour or two in the afternoon. Without establishing my morning routine first and then adding this piece I would not have the time freedom and financial independence I have enjoyed for almost a decade.

And know that ultimately, the best morning routine for you is the one that you will adhere to over time. **Make some notes in your journal about this concept and strategy and how it will change your life in a positive way.**

Areas of Your Life

I look in the mirror each morning and ask myself:
'If today were the last day of my life, would I want
to do what I am about to do today?'
And if the answer is 'No' I know I
need to change something.
~ Steve Jobs

Now that you have read about mentoring from my perspective and with examples from my life, let's discuss you and what you are searching for in your relationship with a mentor. First of all, think about the areas of your life where a mentor would be most valuable at this point in time.

Over this last decade I have had mentors for general areas of my life, as well as ones for more specific areas. For example, when I added selling physical products online as a new business model, I sought out a mentor who had vast experience with this. And when I needed more insight into the process of creating a simple information product with several upsells to post on a platform called Warrior Plus, I hired a mentor who had done this successfully more than forty times over the past decade.

Ask yourself what you most need help with today that a mentor would be able to help you with and advise you. These are some areas to consider:

- Health - this could include weight loss, nutrition, fitness, sleep issues, illness, injury, brain health, and other areas. The saying is true that if you don't have your health, nothing else will matter.
- Business - starting a new business, planning for retirement or for the next chapter of your life, generational legacy,

consulting, coaching, mentoring, and more.

- Interpersonal Relationships - between spouses, siblings, employers and employees, neighbors, parents and teens, and any other relationship you can imagine and may be experiencing.
- Personal Development and Spirituality - finding your life's purpose, mindset, goal setting and achieving, and so much more.
- Investments - stocks, bonds, mutual funds, foreign currencies, real estate, and anything else you may consider investing in for profit.
- Authorship - writing a book, eBooks, blogging, instructional courses and programs, and much more.
- Any other area that is important to you, and that does not fit in to any of the categories I have mentioned here. These could include hobbies, sports, pieces of your business that are more specialized, and travel to exotic lands. In my case, I have sought out mentors to help me learn how to play the ukulele, improve my racquetball game, perfect my public speaking techniques, and get more out of my trips to South America and Asia.

As you can see, this list can be endless as you sort through where you want to begin. And you may have more than one area as your priority right now. I know I am not alone when I say that my life is multi-layered and diverse in my interests and pursuits.

And as you begin to whittle down and refine your own list, think about your goals and priorities in terms of what you wish to accomplishment. Once you have done this, hone in on the exact ways you wish to proceed and then become focused with clarity.

Now it's time to find the right mentor for the area and goals you wish to accomplish.

First, know what you want. Before you approach anyone as a potential mentor, ask yourself:

- *What am I attempting to learn and accomplish? What are my short-term and long-term goals in this area?*
- *Why am I seeking out this particular leader? How can he or she help me achieve those goals I deem important at*

this point in time?
- *Will my core values and beliefs be in alignment with those of this particular mentor?*

At the end of our time together, what will I consider a positive and productive win or a gain from this relationship?

Single-minded, Focused, and with Clarity

I am defining single-minded focus as being the focus on one thing to the exclusion of everything else, for the period of time it will take in order for you to achieve your goal. Few people are able to maintain this type of focus for extended periods of time, and when I add "with clarity" to the requirement even fewer will attempt this effort.

You are different. If you have read this book from page one then you have already set yourself apart in terms of your willingness to do what it takes to succeed and to be open to advice, suggestions, and resources from experts and authorities. So now let's dig in to explore some strategies that will make this a simple process for you.

I will begin by sharing some examples of my own journey with single-minded focus. For years I wanted to become a writer. This began when I was eleven or twelve years old, and I spent many an afternoon after school in my backyard daydreaming about the stories I would write. In my mind they were well thought out, with characters and settings and a plot that made them interesting and logical. They flowed from beginning to end in a way that seemed wise beyond my years. Yet there was always one element missing; I seldom wrote them down!

That's right. It wasn't until I was in college that I would make a more mature and concerted effort at storytelling through the written word. I was at UCLA as an undergraduate when I began taking classes in the television and motion picture arts department. In order to complete the class I was forced to put my ideas into words and present them, first to the class and then to the professor.

I can remember as if it were yesterday hearing my words being read aloud. It was a scene from a screenplay I had written, and two of the other students were acting it out in front of the class. If I would have held that feeling as a pure thought for seventeen seconds, using the "Seventeen Second Rule" I shared with you in a previous chapter, that could have catapulted me to the writing success I was so desperately craving. Instead, once the semester was over I put away my notebook and focused on other aspects of my life.

Fast forward to 2010 and I wanted to write a book to become better known in my online business. I sought out a mentor, someone who had successfully published four books within the previous six years and had a serious discussion about how I would accomplish my goal. We made a plan, I took action, and four months later my first book was published.

What was the difference between the first incident I have shared with you and this one? One thing; having a mentor guide me through the single-minded focus with clarity that made it virtually impossible for me to fail as long as I continued to take daily actions.

Each day I began by doing only what absolutely had to be done before moving on to the writing of my book. I had a plan, an outline, and a daily goal. Even though I struggled with my ideas and getting them into writing at first, the daily exercise of actually doing the writing strengthened that muscle for me. Within a few weeks the words flowed more naturally and I began to look forward to this part of my day as being a joyous one. You can do the same thing in any area of your life once you are committed to this type of single-minded focus with clarity.

Now I do understand that the goal you wish to achieve is not the only activity in your life. You are busy and may have a spouse, children, other friends and family members, a job or career, and other interests and causes that take up your time and energy, both physical and mental. I get it.

What I am suggesting here is that you decide exactly which specific goal you wish to achieve, find a mentor to help you, and then work towards achieving this goal for at least a short period of time every single day. That's correct; I want you t spend a minimum of twenty minutes making effort and progress to get you closer to your goal, *every single day.*

When I came up with the idea for this book, my sixteenth to date, I committed to writing and publishing it within the next three months, maximum. I then committed to spending twenty minutes every single day actively engaged and working on some aspect of it, whether it be writing, researching, interviewing, daydreaming, organizing, blogging on the topic of living the mentored life, speaking or writing with my mentor about this topic, or something else.

And when I say every day, I mean every day. Saturdays, Sundays, holidays, special occasions, every day. Why? Because the feeling you will have after keeping your commitment and seeing it through to completion is one of the best feelings you will ever experience in your life.

You may also work on two goals simultaneously, as long as both of them are not "Big Hairy Audacious Goals" or BHAGs, a term coined by James Collins and Jerry Porras in their 1994 book entitled *Built to Last: Successful Habits of Visionary Companies.* In that context a BHAG encourages companies to define visionary goals that are more strategic and emotionally compelling. Later adopted by entrepreneurs, a BHAG refers to any goal that is top of mind and paramount to your Mission and/or your Vision of your life or business.

Collins and Porras further define this as being a goal that is "clear and compelling, serves as unifying focal point of effort, and acts as a clear catalyst for team spirit. It has a clear finish line, so the organization can know when it has achieved the goal; people like to shoot for finish lines."

Go after your goals with single-minded focus and clarity, and with the help of mentors, and your life will very soon be one that is almost unrecognizable from what you are experiencing today.

Fasting for Focus and Clarity

Over the past year I have experimented with something referred to as intermittent fasting. This is a term used for various diets that cycle between a period of fasting and non-fasting during a defined period. Intermittent fasting can also be used with calorie restriction for weight loss, but here I'm not referring to this strategy in connection with weight loss at all. Instead, this is a concept that may result in greater clarity and focus for your life and your business. Fasting for entrepreneurs is not new and has been discussed for almost two decades now.

My process and ritual has been to fast at least one day each month. I cease all eating and drinking, except for small amounts of water by six in the evening, and do not break my fast until six pm the following day. This is known as a twenty-four hour fast, but many people fast for sixteen or seventeen hours at a time successfully.

By eight or nine o'clock the morning after I have begun, my mind becomes crystal clear, unclouded, and transparent, and I am noticeably more alert than usual. This clarity and focus is the reason I believe that fasting for entrepreneurs is such a valuable experience. And when I sit down to eat at the end of this fast I take it slowly because my body has adjusted and is not starving for nourishment. I typically start with a salad and some vegetables so as to ease back into my regular routine of eating.

Author and entrepreneur Robleh Jama said this:

"Fasting gives me less time to do work. With that said though, fasting is effective in that it forces me to prioritize and do more important things. I run on limited energy, which makes me look closer at the things that I thought were important or urgent. Not everything needs to get done right away. There are things that can wait. But when I am eating on a regular schedule, I just tend to take action rather than think too much about my schedule."

Be willing to give this a try at least once to experience this feeling for yourself and to see if intermittent fasting might become a part of your strategy for increased focus and clarity.

Getting Uncomfortable

Do things that have a chance of being original.
Do everything you can to disrupt your comfort zone.
~ Brian Grazer

I firmly believe that you must experience uncomfortable situations on a regular basis in order to grow as a human being and as an entrepreneur. Once you get into the habit of doing this on purpose, you will welcome the opportunity to get out of your comfort zone and step into your power as a thought leader and as an authority figure in your area of expertise.

Early on in my life experience I discovered that I detested confrontation of any kind. Even the thought of saying what I honestly thought and having someone disagree with me was enough to give me both a headache and a stomach ache. What I did not realize at the time, and would not fully understand until decades later was that my body and my mind were sending me warning signals that I should not have ignored.

It wasn't until I was a brand new teacher that I started to overcome this fear and speak up. I wasn't speaking up for myself as much as I was for my fifth and sixth grade students. We were all being bullied into what I later referred to as the "Friday Education Theft" at the school where I was teaching. Allow me to explain.

Before I arrived at that school, a group of teachers got together and made a pact to not bring any work home with them. They intended to do everything that was required of them during their hours at school, which only included one hour each day when they weren't with their students. Their solution to what they perceived as a problem was to show movies on Fridays and take turns doing their teacher and classroom preparation while one or two of them would stay with the kids during the movie.

If you're shocked at reading this right now, you aren't alone. I could not believe this had been going on for so long.

Being a brand new teacher and also working with what was known as an "Emergency Credential", I reluctantly went along with this for the first two weeks. But I knew it was wrong and on the third Friday I did not participate.

About thirty minutes into my lesson that morning one of the teachers pounded on my door. I gave the class something to work on and stepped outside to speak with her, leaving the door slightly ajar. She started screaming at me and spittle was hitting my cheek. My reaction was to open the door all the way so that my students could hear every word, even the not so nice ones that I thought teachers didn't use, even when they were not with their students.

She stomped away after a few minutes and I went back inside my classroom. I wanted to cry. I wanted to run to the bathroom and wash my face where the spit has touched me. I wanted to then run to my car and drive home and never return. But in that moment I found an inner strength and purpose and knew I had to stand up for my kids.

Something else I will add here is that I was teaching in the inner city of Los Angeles. My kids were from very poor families. Half of them were bused in each day from South Central Los Angeles, meaning that they spent up to three hours each day going to and from school. And this was their choice at that time, as mandatory bussing was long gone in the mid to late 1980s in Los Angeles.

Most of the other students at my school were born in the United States to undocumented parents. This put them in a precarious position because of the political climate over the years. What this meant was that I had few, if any families who complained about anything that went on at school. They were so grateful for the education we provided the majority of the time they did not want to make waves with situations they did not fully comprehend.

So I told my students to put down their pencils and close their books so we could have a talk. I was very honest with them about my thoughts on showing movies and not teaching on Fridays. I asked them if they would prefer to see a movie because they did not have that opportunity enough when they were at home. I told them that if anyone wanted to go to the room where they showed the movies on any particular Friday I would not be upset with them. Then I started writing on the board and explaining the numbers and my thinking on this topic.

I already knew everything I would be teaching them that year, I explained. But this was their year, their opportunity to learn and grow as a student, and to prepare for next year. And if I taught for four days instead of five I would be stealing twenty percent of their education that year. And even worse, I would be stealing directly from them and their families because it was tax money that paid my salary. I had been hired to teach for five days each week, not four, and stealing twenty percent of my paycheck was not right.

A very short discussion ensued, and the result was that my students voted unanimously to learn five days each week for the next nine months. I was bursting with pride and wanted to give them each a big hug, but instead I smiled sweetly and asked them to take out their math books for a lesson on fractions and percentage.

I'd like to tell you that my fear and loathing of confrontation disappeared after that day, but that was not the case. Instead, it seemed as though I was facing more confrontation and adversity than ever before. The difference now was that I was willing to stand up for my beliefs.

During those years I was on my own, with no mentor to guide me as to what to say and do in those types of situations. I like to look back and imagine how different my life could have been if that had been the case. Perhaps I am more appreciative of living the mentored life because I came to it so late in life.

Get Out of Your Comfort Zone

As an online entrepreneur I am able to work from home in either of the cities I live in, or from wherever in the world I happen to be. I have worked from airport lounges, internet cafes, the homes of friends and family members, exclusive private clubs, and public libraries. I have done this throughout the United States, as well as in Canada, Mexico, the United Kingdom, Italy, Sweden, Finland, the Netherlands, Thailand, China, and on many islands in the middle of the Caribbean Ocean.

I am most comfortable working from home, and each time I set up my laptop and engage in an activity for my work in a strange and new place I am just a little bit uncomfortable. The further from home and the more different from what I am used to, the more uncomfortable it is for me. And that is exactly why I seek out these opportunities and embrace them fully each time. Allow me to explain.

It takes very little courage to do what you have been doing and have always done. As humans we tend to get set in our ways and resistant to even the most minor change. No matter how old we are, we crave the routine of what we know is safe and good enough for our wants and needs in every area of our lives. And when something happens to upset our apple cart, we are not happy about it at all.

The rub comes when you make a conscious decision to change something in your life. Saying that you want to live in another city, work at a different job, start a business, or anything else is quite different from actually making a plan and taking the steps to make it happen. So if you are finding yourself at a crossroads right now, take a small step back and explore what part of this is making you uncomfortable. Is it the fear of the unknown, your lack of resources, being judged by others, a lack of confidence, or something else? Once you can identify the source of the discomfort you can work through it to alleviate the pain and emerge successful. The goal with this is to take inspired action to accomplish what you set out to do in a focused way.

Daily Self-Talk...Keep It Positive!
I did not understand either the power or the danger of self-talk until mine almost sabotaged the business I was starting in 2006. See if you can relate to any of what I am sharing with you here.

When I first resigned from my classroom teaching job and gave away my best and longest real estate clients I was feeling elated about finally being an entrepreneur. This euphoria lasted for several weeks, where I would begin each day by listening to or watching some training on my computer, reading some relevant information, and then writing a two hundred fifty or so word post to one or more of the blogs I had set up on different topics.

This work would be completed by ten o'clock or so and I would then leave my house for much of the remainder of the day, going about my errands, appointments, and exploration of the new city I was living in and doing as I pleased. Because I was now an entrepreneur and calling the shots in my own business, I could see no harm in spending my time in this way.

At some point the reality of what I was doing each day set in. I wasn't earning any income, and I had also taken on many expenses related to my new business, some of which I did not need but could not see at that time because of my lack of experience and guidance by a mentor.

This is when the negative self-talk began. It started in the morning, as soon as my feet would hit the floor. On the way to my bathroom I would begin telling myself that I couldn't do this - "this" being defined as creating a successful online business that would allow me to work from home and earn enough income to pay my bills. Remember I shared with you earlier that my prayer had been to "meet all of my financial obligations from home, with grace and ease."

One day the bright light came on and I realized exactly what I was doing. I then made accentuating positive self-talk and eliminating negative self-talk a priority in my life.

Most likely I had never engaged in purposeful, positive self-talk, as I hadn't the slightest idea where to begin with this. So I set out to find a way to make this work in my life.

I thought back to a book I had read long ago and discovered it had been updated and released. It's by Dr. Shad Helmstetter and titled *What to Say When You Talk to Yourself.* This book had been so helpful to me while I was going through some difficult situations at a school where I was teaching at the time and I ordered a copy of the new version and dug right it. This was the right place for me to begin my journey of being aware and focusing on positive self-talk.

First thing every morning I would look myself in the mirror and say out loud "You look beautiful. Today you will reach people all over the world with your writing and training. Someone is waiting to hear what only you can say and this will change their life in a positive way."

What sounded so weird and unnatural in the beginning soon became comfortable and necessary. Sometimes I would be in front of my computer and find myself saying something out loud about how important the work I was doing could be to people who would connect with me to learn and grow their businesses. I am now a proponent of ongoing conversations with yourself where you use self-talk to motivate yourself to creating even greater work than you are now doing.

Challenges From Your Mentor

Once you begin working with a mentor, they will challenge you on a regular basis to do more. This may be either a formal or an informal challenge, and the more experienced mentors will present it to you in such a way that you will believe it was your original idea and even up the stakes for the challenge.

For example, during the first year I was working online as an entrepreneur I saw that my mentors were writing and publishing many blog posts and articles, both on their own sites and on the articles directories that were popular at that time. After a couple of discussions as to the value of writing and publishing regularly on your topic, I came up with the idea (see, I still believe it was my original idea) to challenge myself to write one hundred articles in one hundred days.

You may have heard about this challenge if you have been following me for any time at all. I did not write one hundred articles in one hundred days.

...I wrote one hundred articles in only seventy-eight days!

This led to a variety of opportunities and opened my mind up to new and greater possibilities, for it was on this day that the seed was planted that I could write and publish a book. So on that spring day over a decade ago now I wrote one article, two hundred and fifty words in length that gave me the belief and confidence to keep writing and to move forward with a goal and dream I had held since I was very young.

Since that time mentors have challenged me to host live events and workshops, start my own publishing company, take a cross country road trip to visit clients, friends, and family and to up my life's game in a way I could not and would not have had the wherewithal to do on my own.

It's time to take out your journal or notebook again. Make a list of what you want to change in your life at this time. Do not hold back, as this list will represent your true inner feelings, thoughts, and beliefs about your life experience. Next, have a serious conversation with your spouse, partner, or significant other to share what you are thinking at this time. This is a crucial piece of the puzzle, and if overlooked at this early stage can lead to consequences and repercussions that could backfire and unwind the hard work you are doing.

Finally, spend time with your mentor to go through each step of the process that will be involved as you begin your personal journey of change and growth.

What's Next?

The best and most beautiful things in the world
cannot be seen or even touched
- they must be felt with the heart.
~ Helen Keller

Having mentors in your life gives you an entirely different perspective on everything you do, as well as opportunities you may not have realized were available to you. My best friend growing up had the given name "Mentor", so I knew from an early age this word meant *teacher and trusted advisor*. It wasn't until I was out of college and well into adulthood that I understood and took advantage of the ability to have mentors in my own life. These days I both mentor others and am mentored, and the results have been nothing less than spectacular for everyone involved.

How can you take full advantage of mentoring, and choose to live the mentored life this year and beyond? Here are some questions to ask yourself as you make this transition from attempting to do everything by yourself to allowing a teacher and trusted advisor to guide you to the results and goals you seek to achieve.

- *What do I want and need to learn to take me to the next level in my desired area of life or business?*
- *Who do I currently know that is already an expert in this area, and has achieved this goal themselves?*
- *What is the next logical step for me in this process of working with a mentor?*

More than likely you already have a good idea of what it is you would like to achieve. Perhaps you want to finally write that book others have been telling you to write. Maybe you want to become more proficient with computers and technology, or playing chess, or writing a play, or with line dancing. These three are all areas I have pursued over the past decade and ones where a mentor made it all so much faster and easier for me to achieve the results I was hoping to master.

A good mentor is honest with you about everything; what you need to do to get started, how you are progressing, when it is time to do it on your own. Being mentored is much like being a baby bird, cared for by a skilled and loving mother bird and then abruptly being shoved out of the nest to fly or sink like a rock. But unlike the aviary community, a great mentor will catch you as you fall, spreading out their arms to glide you safely back to where you need to be at this point in time.

In return, you must trust and be honest with anyone who mentors you. If you are experiencing fear or doubt around the goals you are working to achieve, schedule a time to discuss this with them. If you find yourself taking a turn towards another goal instead of completing the one they advised you on, let them know you're having second thoughts and wish to make a change in the direction you are going right now. They will be the one person best able to advise you, based on the relationship the two of you have been building over time.

For now, make a list of what you wish to achieve during the first part of 2018. Open up your mind and dream big! If I hadn't been willing to do this starting in 2006, I would not be the author of more than a dozen bestselling books. What do you want as a part of your life experience that right now seems like it is too big for you to say out loud? Get in front of a mirror, look yourself in the eyes, and say it to yourself, for once you have expressed your desires the next step is finding someone to mentor you to completion and success.

Once you let it be known that you need help with a specific goal, the mentor will appear. When you can trust in this process the magic truly begins. Imagine what this year can bring when you are willing to live the mentored life and finally reach, and even exceed your own potential. I'd love to hear from you on this topic. Sharing your goals and dreams out loud is an effective part of this process that leads to excellent results.

Beyond the Mentor

Let us remember: One book, one pen, one child, and
one teacher can change the world.
~ Malala Yousafzai

When my own mentors began having conversations with me about moving "beyond the mentor" I was confused. if the goal was to improve all aspects of our lives by living the "mentored life", then why would we ever consider moving beyond our mentors? Through a variety of strategies and over a period of weeks with someone I will introduce to you here, I came to understand exactly what my mentors meant and to then embrace this concept wholeheartedly.

If you subscribe to the belief that the universe is infinite, as are all of the events it is comprised of, then it stands to reason that all things are possible and that we have only seen and experienced the tip of the iceberg when it comes to what we can achieve during our lifetimes. If nothing ever ends but simply circles around to an ever widening and deeper space, we must think in terms of moving beyond what is currently working for us, in a way that honors the present and anticipates even greater occurrences in the future.

My first concrete experience with someone who had moved beyond mentors was with a man I met in Santa Barbara in 2014. He and his wife were at a meeting I attended for some issues we were facing in the community that required massive fundraising and immediate action. We were immediately attracted to one another based on our views and reactions to what was being discussed and quickly became fast friends.

A few days later we were enjoying a dinner of local cuisine at the Finch & Fork, a restaurant in downtown Santa Barbara known for its simple elegance. I was not surprised they had chosen this location for our first meeting and for the purpose of getting to know one another better.

John asked me about my business before I could ask him about his, and I proceeded to share my story of going from employee of the school district in Los Angeles and part-time real estate broker and residential appraiser to that of an author, publisher, and entrepreneur. I waited to see his reaction, and it was his wife Betty who spoke first.

"What have you written? Would I have heard about it?"

I smiled and slowly withdrew two of my recent books from my handbag.

"I don't believe so," I said and handed one book to each of them.

For the next several minutes they looked through my books, trading with each other at some point and then trading back once again so that both could peruse each of the titles I had shared with them. It was a graceful and respectful dance, and something I took note of for the next time anyone gave me one of their books in person.

We then engaged in a three hour discussion, punctuated by the detailed timing of our salads, dinners, and desserts. I know I was smiling wider than I normally do, as it felt as though I had entered a different realm and was outside of my body.

We discussed anything and everything and I came to know that John was a venture capitalist and Betty was his assistant and bookkeeper. They were involved with projects of various types around the world, but preferred to work on more local projects as of late. They did not give me names or specifics because privacy was a major concern. This made me feel comfortable because I knew they would do the same with any information I shared about my own business.

After mentioning Rotary several times that evening, John finally acknowledged me by asking if I knew a few people whom he named. Yes, all of them were in my Club. I asked if he ever attended Rotary meetings, as there are eight separate Clubs in the greater Santa Barbara area.

The conversation that ensued was an enlightening one for me. It was on this evening when I learned a lesson about a life beyond mentors, at least as I was defining them and had experienced for almost a decade at that point in my life.

John led the discussion, pausing politely at times to allow me to gather my thoughts and add a comment or ask a question. I knew his words were life changing and would not have dared to interrupt or to contradict him until I had heard him out. This was yet another of the special and unique times in my life where I know I have been subjected to the thoughts and ideas of someone who has a perspective worth exploring in a serious way.

He explained that there are times in our lives where we must move forward boldly, even if we know we are not quite ready. Sometimes we take a job or enter a career or have a life experience that catapults us into a new world, a world unfamiliar and even possibly quite frightening for us. I related this to my first day as a student at UCLA, my first day as a classroom teacher, and the first day I woke up as an novice entrepreneur who no longer had the safety net of a job with a salary and paid medical plan.

John then shared his thoughts on Rotary and other service organizations, from the perspective of those who remain members for life, as well as those who move on to others avenues of service to those in need around the world.

I listened intently once again as he told me that to be a true thought leader and to make changes in the world we must take the lead. To only participate in established groups and organizations was to miss out on the opportunity to have your own Mission and Vision come to fruition. He shared his take on the people who started some of the world' greatest charitable organizations and non-profit foundations, like Paul Harris did with Rotary in 1905 and the Boys & Girls Club, originally founded in 1860 by Elizabeth Hamersley and sisters Mary and Alice Goodwin. These are but two examples of the great work done by caring people. But even if one was to devote their life to carrying out the great work of groups such as these, as I was doing at the time, it is still limiting one's own potential, should you choose to accept this as a goal.

Then I got it! That's when my eyes lit up and I jumped in to the conversation with a renewed understanding of my own life's purpose. It was noble to be involved with the half dozen or so groups I had connected with over the past decade, and to serve them in ways that allowed me to share my ideas and skills, but it was incumbent on me to go further and to do more.

The precept that we must move "beyond our mentors" in order to fully give back to the world and to expand the thinking and the opportunities for others who have a heart for the issues we care about was now crystal clear in my mind.

This did not mean that I needed to resign from any of the groups I was currently a member of; nothing could be further from that. No, instead my new goal was to dig deep inside and discover my innermost passion around serving others and then take the lead in making my dream become a reality.

So I asked myself two questions:

What is my passion for serving others?

How will I become a thought leader in order to bring about true change in this area?

I'm still working on this part of my life, but I can share with you that this will be around working with children who are living in poverty. I was one of those children and understand firsthand what it does to your confidence and sense of worth. Each day I think about this and am getting closer to stepping in to my power to enact a vehicle in which to deliver my program for change. In the meantime I continue to work closely with the people and organizations that are already doing great work in this area so that I will know more and be further aware of what is needed.

The final step in going beyond your mentors is to become a mentor to others. This does not mean that you no longer need to be mentored yourself, but instead means that you are ready to guide others in their own journey to mastery, deeper understanding, and service to others.

Now it's your turn to answer the two questions I offered above and write about them in your journal. Once again, they are:

- *What is my passion for serving others?*
- *How will I become a thought leader in order to bring about true change in this area?*

Creating Something Bigger

There are more and more entrepreneurs that think big.
Many will fail, but the ones who succeed
will change the world.
~ Steve Jurvetson

It is my sincere belief that we must only take a short pause to be content along the points of light we achieve, and then leap forward in a way that will forever stretch us to think and become bigger than we are at the current moment.

For most of my life I spent time with people who laughed out loud when I expressed my dreams and goals to them. It did not take long before I stopped telling them anything, but simultaneously I stopped thinking and dreaming big on my own. I should have continued the conversation in my mind, without sharing it out loud. But hindsight is 20/20 in that events that occur are obvious later on that were not so at the onset and the choices we made might well have been more reactionary than based on rational thoughts and actions.

In other words, I allowed others to stop me in my tracks for several decades. This was based on my fears - the fear of failure, of success, of ridicule and criticism, and of feeling that I was not good enough to achieve even a modicum of true success. It was only when the pain of not doing what my heart and mind yearned for was far greater than the pain of staying where I was that I was finally willing to get out of my own way and change my life completely. I hope that your journey has not been as painful as mine was for so many years, but no matter where you were and where you are now you are ready to create something much bigger in your life.

Anything is possible as long as you are willing to do the work and reap the rewards.

Your First Steps

Before you move forward, take some time to reflect on where you are today and where you wish to move towards from today on. You notice I did not say where you will be in one year or in five years, but where you wish to be after you reflect on your current status. This is because the future will always be a moving target, one that requires ongoing thought and course correction. And there is no ideal length of time or date in the future for which you must complete your goals. Instead, think of today as the day you begin your journey to create a life bigger than you have ever created in the past. No matter what you have already accomplished and achieved, there is something much bigger waiting for you on the other side.

A mentor who is in tune with you and your core values will introduce you to the idea of focused intention. I have written on this topic in the past, most recently in my last book, *Rethinking the Work Ethic: Embrace the Struggle and Exceed Your Own Potential*. Here I will expound upon what I have said previously in a way that will make sense for our current topic of living the mentored life.

Living each moment in focused intention requires a clarity of purpose and a trust in the process of positive change and accelerated growth in your life. Once you understand and accept the power of this principle your days will flow more smoothly and you will effortlessly achieve your goals. Allow me to explain what I am referring to with this statement more clearly and succinctly.

We have already discussed the importance of having a morning routine, where you ease into your day with clarity and purpose. Now let's take those precepts to the next level by being intentional with each thought and action you take throughout the day. I will use my morning as an example.

Today I have just returned from spending almost a week in Phoenix, Arizona where I stayed with friends while attending a live event with more than two thousand people in attendance. As an introvert this is quite an undertaking, but I am committed to fulfilling my goals and dreams regardless of the circumstances. My time was quite enjoyable and well spent. The drive home was several hours longer than expected due to heavy traffic coming back into southern California, as well as an accident that closed Interstate 10 and rerouted us through the back roads of Arizona coming into California.

Needless to say, I was quite exhausted by the time I arrived home last night and into this morning. On the way home yesterday I set the intention to get a good night's sleep and to sleep for one to two hours later than usual this morning. I accomplished that and my next intention was to write more on this book for sixty to ninety minutes. Because I keep a document with my notes on the book I am currently writing, along with the document that will become my book, I am able to pick up from where I left off, eight days ago in this case, without skipping a beat.

I am now an hour into todays writing and enjoying the process immensely, as I hope that you are as well as the reader. Right now my only focus is on the writing. I have several more items of importance to complete before the end of today, but for now I could not even tell you what they are because I am intentionally focused on writing. I hope this makes sense to you. In a way, it's as if the whole world is going on without me because I am not needed by anyone or anything, nor do I wish to be anywhere else right now. This frees up my mind for what I consider to be my most important task, that of writing this chapter and feeling the joy of doing so.

Remember that your goal is to create something bigger than what you have been creating as a part of your life experience. This requires not only bigger thinking and actions but also trust on a deeper level than you may be accustomed to as a part of your life experience. This trust in the process may be the most difficult part of your journey, but it fits in perfectly with what is possible when you are guided by a mentor in the direction of achieving your goals and dreams.

This is all a part of listening to your intuition. I have discovered that visualizing your goals is an important part of this process.

When you visualize anything, it makes it much more likely for you to turn it into a reality. You first see the vision in your head and then take steps to make it happen. Think of the people you consider to be visionaries, such as Steve Jobs, who pictured how his products could help improve peoples' lives and Thomas Edison, who spent years improving and perfecting the light bulb.

Visualizing your goals carries through on this same concept in a two part process. First you paint a picture of what you would like to accomplish by a certain date. When you have that picture clearly in your mind, you can then determine what steps and action is necessary in order to implement it.

Once you break down the steps to accomplish your goals, you can use other visualization tools and techniques to help you manage those steps. Earlier in this book in the chapter on finding mentors I shared the *Seventeen Second Rule* with you, and this is yet another visualization strategy that is effective for successful change and productivity.

Write everything down in a notebook if that works best for you, or you may simply choose to keep track of your tasks in a spreadsheet or other document. Keep using whatever tool is working.

Many times I have also created a vision board. My technique involves cutting out pictures from magazines or printing relevant images from the internet. This has been quite powerful for me over the years. Again, there are no rules or requirements here. If you understand your vision, then it's the right one for you.

You may wish to incorporate all the concepts above or use only a few. You must experiment to see which ones most resonate with you. It's an iterative process. However, the key is not to get caught up in the process itself. Whatever means you use to visualize your goals, you need to make sure you track the progress. Otherwise, you are simply going through the motions, and you will not accomplish very much.

The last of these "first steps" is the daily practice of gratitude. I don't know how many years I heard others speaking about this before I made it a part of my life. At first I thought it simply meant to thank God for the people and situations that blessed my life, but now I understand it to be a more involved practice, where we move throughout each day with a sense of reverence of and gratefulness for our lives.

Each morning as I am going through the rituals I shared earlier in the chapter on "Morning Routine" I take the time to write down and say out loud what I am grateful for in my life. Today I am grateful for a safe journey back from Phoenix, the clear skies and warm temperatures of this first week of spring, and for the people I met at the live event this past week who are now a part of my life experience.

But I take the time to go on from those words to a deeper and more meaningful expression of my gratitude. Remember that we are seeking something bigger in our lives, and bigger means more details, expectations, and commitments to ourselves and to others.

I go on to think about how I felt during my drive back to California. What did that experience mean to me and how would I change it in the future? Did I simply site in the car and drive west for four hundred miles or did I engage in deep thoughts as least part of this time? What did I learn that could help me and others, now and on an ongoing basis?

And it is the first week of spring, something that was important enough for me to mention when I was expressing gratitude this morning. What could I do today and this week that would not only be possible, and also enhanced because of the weather? Perhaps I could invite some of the people I have gone walking with in the past to join me in the local park (the one I frequent in Santa Clarita is called Central Park and the one in Santa Barbara is called Arroyo Burro) for an hour of walking, talking, and brainstorming.

As for the people I spent time with in Phoenix, both the friends I stayed with and those who were also in attendance at the live event, how will I follow up with them to further deepen and strengthen our relationships? Each person is special and unique and deserves to achieve their goals and dreams. Is there a way for me to facilitate their process with my words, actions, or in some other way?

Take a few minutes right now to write down in your journal the three first steps I have shared here, those being focused intention, visualization, and daily gratitude. Trust in the process and know that anything is possible. If you are already working with one or more mentors, share this process and your experience with them and include them in your journey to create something bigger.

Note: I introduced the concept of core values earlier in this book, as well as within this chapter. I asked thought leader Sue Guiher to share more with us on this topic and this is included at the end of the book in the Addendum.

Giving Back

*Help others to achieve their dreams and
you will achieve yours.*
~ Les Brown

I waited until I had gone beyond six figures a year, replacing my previous income as a classroom teacher and real estate broker and appraiser with my new endeavor as an online entrepreneur before I began taking people into a mentor program. In my mind this was the right thing to do at that time, even though no one told me it was necessary to wait.

At the time I was simply more concerned with being authentic and truthful when serving others, and achieving the milestone of earning more than a hundred thousand dollars a year made sense if I were to be guiding others towards this goal. My dream was to give back in this way. Giving back refers to the process of taking people under your wing and guiding them toward the success they wish to achieve.

Why I Call It Mentoring

As I have progressed as an entrepreneur since 2006 I have made an intense study of what occurs when someone begins working with a coach or mentor. And I will note here that from the very beginning the people I have worked with online and experienced the greatest growth with refer to themselves as mentors.

In my mind, and I realize this is only my perception, a coach is someone who cheers you on, shares more tactics and strategies with you, and tells you that you can do it. "It" is whatever your goals are at that particular time.

On the other hand, a mentor gets to know you on a deeper level, listens as you share your thoughts, ideas, and dreams, and then develops a unique strategy just for you that encompasses not only what you set out to achieve, but also what your mentor sees that you can achieve. They take you under their wing, pushing you to the edge of what they know is possible for you, then gently catching you if you fall short at any point along the way. They promote you, challenge you, and create opportunities for you that you might not have ever come upon without them.

I identify as a mentor, and sometimes describe myself as a "stage mother" (in the most positive connotation of this phrase) to those I work closely with every day. My best efforts come when I am able to spend time with my mentee, as well as with other members of their family. Just as I did with the children I taught over a twenty year period, my relationship with a mentee is a holistic one, where we explore and discover heretofore hidden and undisclosed aspects of their life that will be useful as they work to accomplish their goals and dreams. This includes knowing more about their personality, life experiences, education and training, core values and beliefs, and the interactions they have with the people around them.

I have observed some coaches who are actually mentors, like athletic coaches who get to know the families of their players, and academic tutors who spend time with their tutee away from the books and lessons. Many times these coaches will be in the role of friend and authority figure to introduce new experiences and perspectives to the person they are working with. I have seen music teachers work so closely with their students that they become aware of other areas of the arts that will help them with their first instrument. So it is possible for these terms of coach and mentor to be interchangeable in certain situations.

Reread Denise Wakeman's foreword to this book to hear her take and understanding of this distinction between coaches and mentors. She and I are in agreement on this, even though we have never specifically discussed it over the years. Perhaps her mentoring helped to shape my thoughts and ideas around this topic, as often is the case when you are mentored by someone over a period of years.

In any case, having that special person or people in your life to guide you along the path that most closely resonates with your hopes, dreams, desires, and goals is one you do not want to miss out on during your lifetime.

Giving Back with Mentoring

Most likely you are already mentoring someone, whether you think of it in this way or not. What I am suggesting here is that you do this on purpose and on a regular basis to share what you have learned along your life's journey with others.

Mentoring others is about building confidence while also guiding creativity. This duality was covered extensively in a book I co-wrote with the late, great Geoff Hoff, entitled *The Inner Game of Internet Marketing*.

Fostering confidence in others, which I define as your belief in yourself and in your belief in your ability to be capable and to figure things out on your own can be the greatest gift you ever bestow upon another human being. Some are fortunate to have received this gift while growing up, while the rest of us must achieve it on an ongoing basis throughout adulthood. Either way, a confident person is highly competent and successful, and a joy to spend time with when they are living their truth and reaching out to others.

Guiding creativity is a process of taking someone from where they are today with the goals and dreams they wish to achieve, to a place where they can create their life's journey through a variety of exercises and activities that will allow them to experience a full mind shift. Unleashing this creative side, something common to all human beings will ensure that the people you mentor receive the full measure of what you have to offer.

And, as stated so eloquently by Les Brown, in the quote I shared at the beginning of this chapter, when you help others to achieve their dreams you will achieve yours. To date I have worked personally with more than a thousand people, and in each situation I have learned and grown as much as they have. It becomes a symbiotic relationship where each of you benefit from the ongoing interactions over time. I have even engaged in the Socratic method with my mentees, where we ask and answer questions to stimulate critical thinking and to draw out ideas that lie just beneath the surface. The results have been phenomenal and have led to greater confidence and creativity in our ability to build lucrative and satisfying businesses.

Conclusion

When your values are clear to you,
making decisions becomes easier.
~ Roy E. Disney

It has been a joyous process to share what living the mentored life can mean to your life's journey. By this time, if you have read through from the beginning of this book you are thinking differently about the relationships you have with the people in your life who mentor you, as well as those you have with the people you continue to mentor.

In speaking with a long time friend recently, we both shared how we felt that we did not have people to help us with various situations and goals as we were growing up. We came to the conclusion that this was not an accurate account of what had occurred all those years ago. We have reframed this memory to be one where we took the lead with what we wanted to achieve on our own, and the right people showed up in our lives to assist us with the details along the way.

I have discussed what living the mentored life means, why it's important to be mentored, the possibilities when you have mentors in various areas, and how you will live once you are leading the mentored life. We then explored what comes next in terms of creating something bigger in your life and giving back by mentoring others in areas of strength for you.

I want you to think about your experiences with mentorship in relation to what you have already achieved, as well as what you wish to achieve in the future. Go back through these pages and make notes in your journal as to what is important to you right now and who could most help you to move closer to your goals. This is a journey, not a destination, and that is even more exciting as you move confidently down the road of your choosing. Being present during the course of your life will empower you as you move forward.

Now I hope you will indulge me as I think out loud, at least here in this writing about something I am now referring to as the five prongs of a successfully mentored life. I predict this will become the topic of another book at some point, so for now I am sharing an early preview of my thinking in this area. It is directly related to living the mentored life and may enhance your knowledge and spark new ideas you may be willing to share with your community.

The Five Prongs of a Successfully Mentored Life
At the beginning of the earlier section on how to live the mentored life I shared my thoughts on the pieces that comprise your ability to live in this way. Again, these pieces are:

Communication
Implementation
Innovation
Discipline
Persuasion

These five concepts, taken individually and in unison, and fleshed out into meaningful, relevant ideas become at once the playground and the laboratory of the mind. Allow me to explain my hypothesis more fully.

The seed of an idea, once planted and germinated and pushed up through the earth into the light of day deserves to come to fruition as a world vision for all to enjoy and benefit from. This is my belief and my hope is that you will agree, at least in part as to its relevance and importance for the human condition to evolve in this new millennium.

You may already agree that communication, clear and well thought out, is absolutely necessary to intelligent human beings and furthering our culture of growth. Even though our communication methods have changed outwardly since the dawn of mankind, when you peel back the layers the premise is still the same. The ability to share ideas from one mind to another and back again is crucial to change and growth within civilizations.

But communication alone does not scale mountains or cross rivers. We must practice implementation as a daily ritual to expand our communication into viable actions, processes, and the basis of positive and forward change.

Implementing the thoughts and ideas we communicate can become stale and stagnant if we do not come up with innovative ways to make what we have learned through our communications unique. Innovation paves the way for thought leaders and thinkers in all disciplines to share their innermost thoughts and ideas with lay people worldwide.

These concepts repeated once and then forgotten end the chain of sharing higher level thoughts and ideas with our fellow man. By developing the discipline to engage in the implementation and innovation of the communications that are shared with us, we ensure the ongoing journey of these activities throughout our lifetimes. Discipline ensures that the ideas, beliefs, and values are carried forward and shared in a variety of ways over time so as to become a part of the collective thinking of all people, with each person having the power to add to, dissent from, and express their opinion on an equal footing.

And all of this is for naught if we do not improve and engage in the art of persuasion to make sure all people are included. Persuasion, as stated and intended here allows for people in all corners of the world to become a part of the conversation that may ultimately dictate portions of their daily life experiences. My thought is that this piece may level the playing field in some way that will make a difference to someone who has previously been left out or marginalized.

It is your task, if you choose to accept, to become a thought leader in your field of interest and expertise in order to bring these concepts and the five-pronged approach to fruition.

As your final journal entry for the ideas and concepts included in this book, share your thoughts and feelings on this five pronged approach to a successfully mentored life.

How will you help to impact change in our world, using this model of mentorship?

What type of foundation must you lay in order to affect the people around you?

Which prongs of this idea do you most resonate with, and which ones would you develop further in order for your thoughts, beliefs, and core values to be honored?

Who will you seek out to mentor you through the process of becoming a thought leader, in an area of great interest to you and based on your core values and beliefs?

Addendum: Core Values

I asked thought leader Sue Guiher to share her knowledge with us on the topic of core values, a relevant one for you as you consider and move forward with a mentored life.

As you have read in this book, the life of an entrepreneur can be challenging as well as very rewarding. Having a mentor to help guide you and support you along the way is extremely important. Along with finding the right external guide, you must first recognize the guide within you. Every person is born with an internal guidance system that helps them to find their right path, to make the right decisions and to bring the right people into their lives. It is this inner guide that I want to share with you in this chapter.

The inner guide is reflected in your values so that is where we will start. Understanding your core values, who you are and what you want is the key to continually moving forward in life. Most companies have a mission statement which is a reflection of what the company stands for. When they need to make a decision, they lean into their values. Johnson and Johnson has always had the core value of responsibility toward its customers. So in 1982 when Tylenol was found to be tainted with cyanide, they recalled all of their Tylenol products at the cost of $100 Million. However, they were leaning into their values and have continued to be well-respected. They also went on to be a leader in protective packaging so that an incident like that one would not happen again. They lived up to their core value of responsibility to their customers.

During this chapter, I want to answer a few things for you:
The importance of knowing your Core Values
Difference between Core Values and Aspirational Values
Putting your values into practical use

Why Should You Understand Your Core Values?

You might be thinking, "I am not a big company. My values really don't impact my clients or my work." You could not be farther than the truth. EVERYTHING in your life and your business is impacted by your values. (*Full transparency, MY belief is that your business is part of your life so whenever I speak about something impacting your business, it most likely also impacts your personal life*.)

Values are like a lighthouse meant to direct and guide you through life's journey.

They are also like having a compass in your pocket. When things get confusing, you can pull your values out and use them to reorient yourself and get back on track.

Values help you determine what is most important to you in all aspects of your business and life. Values help define who a person is and help that person determine their life's priorities. The degree of fulfillment a person experiences in life is directly related to whether their important values are honored.

Think back to events in your life when you were living as your *"best self"*. How did you feel? What type of work were you doing? Were you working with a group or on your own? What made you excited to get up in the morning and get to work? What are the "rules" or boundaries you have set for how you want to live your life? (being honest, being loyal, being a hard-worker etc.)

As you begin to answer these questions, you may see a pattern begin to emerge. Often this pattern reflects the value that contributes to our purpose. For example, my purpose is teaching. I could eat, sleep and breathe "teaching" and this is reflected within my values of learning, growth, education. Teaching is one of the reasons my company specializes in personal and business development. My company reflects my values in the services I provide, what products I develop and in my ideal clients, partners and mentors. My company values and my personal values are in alignment and are a pretty strong match.

This is an important point I would like to make. As an entrepreneur, especially a solopreneur, your personal values often will be reflected in your company's values but sometimes they won't be a complete match. You should determine your values and then determine what you value as a business. If you have a partner, each of you should separately identify your values and then determine the values for your company. Most of the time they will match and on occasion, they may not.

For example, perhaps freedom and flexibility are very important values to you. Perhaps your company, however, is involved in providing services that are all about safety and security. Let's say, internet security is what your company does. Your company values may be to provide security solutions that allow our clients to feel safe and secure while doing business on the web. Safety is the core value for your company. Now, your value may be reflected in the way that you provide this service with flexible pricing or by speaking about the freedom that your clients experience because they no longer are worried that their company website is going to be hacked.

What are Aspirational Values?
When you are determining your core values, you may go through many different types of exercises. (At the end of the chapter I have included a link to an exercise for you to explore your core values. This exercise is different than most exercises you may have done before because it goes to a much deeper level.)

Sometimes, we chose values that are really not present on a daily basis but are ones we like and that we "aspire" to have. These are values that a person really wants to be true for them.

They reflect qualities that a person respects and aspires to, but are not currently true for them and as such are called, aspirational values.

Aspirational values are more hope than truth. As such, they help a person imagine something better for themselves.

Aspirational values have another important role. They are very important when looking for a mentor. You have already learned how important it is to work with mentors. But picking the right one can be confusing at times. When looking for a mentor, look for someone whose values are in alignment with your own AND who also has the values you are aspiring to have. Mentors act as models as well as guides. If they already demonstrate a value you are aspiring to have, then ask them about it and use their wisdom to help you grow.

Values are not static and they do change as we grow, learn, and change. They also can change as a result of a person, situation or environment. You can change as you grow. Understanding what you value at each level of growth will help you to continue to move forward and live as your best self.

Using Your Values

We already talked about how knowing your values can create a guide for how you want to act in your business. We also covered how to hire a mentor based on what are your core values as well as your aspiration values. So how do we use values in our everyday life?

One way of doing this is my creating a "Value Statement". Remember that we talked about companies having a "Mission Statement" that reflects their values. For me, I like having a "Value Statement". Having a value statement can help you make the best choices for you and your business.

A Value Statement is a statement of who you are and how you will interact with the world around you. Your value statement will govern the way you choose to live and conduct yourself. It will help you to make decisions that are in alignment with what you truly believe and how you want to show up in the world.

By living by your values, you can experience greater success and fulfillment both personally and professionally. I invite you to learn more about yourself by creating your Thriving Core Values Profile. This complimentary, short exercise (less than 30 minute) will help you to understand what values are truly important to you. It is the first step in creating your inner GPS system.

Go now to **www.thrivingentrepreneur.com/values-for-living-the-mentored-life** and find out for yourself.

I have so much information about living your best life according to your values that I will send you some other resources when you sign up to go through the Core Values Exercise.

About the Author

Wouldn't take nothing for my journey now.
~ Maya Angelou

Connie Ragen Green is an online marketing strategist, bestselling author, international speaker, and mentor to people on six continents. She is a former classroom teacher, real estate broker, and residential appraiser who left it all behind to start an online business during 2006.

This change of direction with career, lifestyle, and goals occurred as she came to realize that she wanted something more from her life than what she was currently experiencing. This was the beginning of a new life, where anything is possible and everything unfolds in a magical way.

After struggling during her first year of entrepreneurship, Connie finally embraced the struggles of writing and technology, leveled up her work ethic, carefully chose her mentors, and continues to exceed her own potential in her life and business.

Making her home in two cities, Santa Barbara, California at the beach and Santa Clarita, California in the desert, Connie is active with a number of charities, non-profits, and service organizations. These include Rotary, an international service organization; Zonta, a women's business organization with the Mission of advancing the status of women worldwide; the Benevolent and Protective Order of Elk; the Boys and Girls Clubs of America; and SEE International, an organization dedicated to restoring the vision of people in underdeveloped countries.

Becoming an online entrepreneur changed Connie's life forever. Once she became versed in online marketing and observed first-hand how powerful the effect was for people all over the world, she began writing on a variety of topics, creating information products, speaking at live events and workshops, and mentoring people on how to build a successful and lucrative business they can run from home or from anywhere in the world. She also works with corporations in the area of online marketing and sales strategies.

Find out more and receive some relevant information right away by visiting **https://connieragengreen.com** to further connect with Connie and to begin your own journey of online entrepreneurship.